... from this .

GHOST TOWN
Album

By
Lambert Florin

Maps and Drawings
by
David C. Mason, M.D.

Bonanza Books • New York

517R01403

COPYRIGHT MCMLXII BY SUPERIOR PUBLISHING COMPANY, SEATTLE, WASHINGTON

This edition published by Bonanza Books
a division of Crown Publishers, Inc.
by arrangement with Superior Publishing Company

b c d e f g h

Library of Congress Card Number 62-21937

Printed in the United States of America

DEDICATION

GHOST TOWN ALBUM
is dedicated to my mother
NANNY MARIE FLORIN
who loved to poke around in
old abandoned houses

FOREWORD

Ghost town fever affects many people in the same way gambling does but perhaps not with such an extreme compulsion. And the rewards are every bit as uncertain. What lies around that last bend in the road? Will there be a double row of little false-fronted stores lining a grassy street or only a few piles of rubbish and tins cans to mark the spot where gold-hungry throngs lived, loved and died? Or, sadly enough, will the scene be graced by a shiny new filling station, garish "authentic" restorations of saloons with rows of slot machines?

In the first book of this series, Western Ghost Towns, I related how Dr. David Mason and I happened to become interested in old camps, the places where so much human life had been lived in lusty fashion. I gave an idea of our wonderings as to where the people who occupied the old houses and did business in the old stores and danced the nights away in the old honky tonks . . . where they had all gone . . . how many were still lying in the desolate, often unmarked graves over on the side of the hill.

It so happened Dr. Mason and I were on our way to our respectives homes after a joint vacation spent mountain climbing, fishing and alpine plant collecting in the High Sierra of California. We had saved out a day's time to visit an old mining camp we had heard about casually—Bodie. Fortunately our first example of a ghost town was an ideal one. Bodie's silent streets and red-hued, false-fronted buildings cast an immediate spell, one lasting to the point where the hobby of mountain climbing was shelved, temporarily I hope. I'd like to think there will be time for both activities in the future.

Worth repeating also is our definition of a ghost town. My dictionary has no listing of such an item but it does give several definitions for "ghost," one of which is beautifully applicable to our purpose: "a shadowy semblance of its former self." Not all the towns pictured in the series are dead and so cannot be shadowy semblances; they cover all stages in the process of fading away. Perhaps the extreme example of a town's demise would be Battle, Wyoming. The town has not only been completely abandoned but its remaining buildings were considered a "fire trap" and the CCC boys ordered to destroy them.

At the other end of the span we would cite Jamestown, California. Intimately known as "Jimtown," it is currently thriving and not at all like it was in the days of the Gold Rush. Yet at the same time Jamestown is a shadowy semblance and redolent of the days of '49. All the towns included in the series lie in between these extremes, some making gallant comebacks, all full of history and worth visiting for a look at whatever might be reminiscent of the roistering old days.

Painfully evident to the sensitive observer is the fact that any historical evidence remaining is fast disappearing. Time is the worst depradator but vandals, both by motive and accident, come a close second. I have seen people loading bricks into their cars, precious relics plucked out of the fragile walls of some remaining gem of early architecture in the Mother Lode country. One of them asked flippantly: "Who's going to miss a couple of bricks?" He didn't realize he is only one of many visitors and if each took "a couple of bricks" there would quickly be nothing left of the landmark.

Wagon wheels seem to have an irresistible attraction for many people with acquisitive natures. In the old carriage shed at Granite, Montana, are several beautiful examples of buggies used in the '80s. Each of these rests ignominiously on the dusty floor, shorn of its graceful wheels. There is also the unwanted individual who carelessly tosses his cigarette butt near a pile of tinder dry boards. Endless numbers of historic frame structures have gone up in smoke in a matter of moments from this cause alone.

Imagine the thrill any ghost town fan would feel if he were to find a house intact, with all its furnishings in place, just as its long-gone inhabitants left it. Many homes were abandoned in this fashion, furniture and other articles not removed for one reason or another, but precious few have retained these mementos. An old couple we talked to in Kelly, New Mexico, said: "We find people even carrying away the headboards from the cemetery and we're worried they'll be digging up the bodies next. You wouldn't publicize these old towns if you knew what the souvenir hunters do to us."

There are a few souvenirs to be collected legitimately and with good taste, I believe. Often one runs across square-headed, hand-forged nails in the road and these are much more socially acceptable in the enthusiast's home than in his tires. Sometimes he will be lucky enough to find an article of glass which has turned purple in years of sunshine. If this is not in a house or shed but out in the brush or grass, a person would certainly have the right to take it home.

The pursuit of old abandoned towns offers many incidental rewards. The searcher is led along obscure byways, most of them not frequented by the average motorist. Often he will find it advantageous to camp in or near his goal to take advantage of the morning light for photographs or sketches. And there is nothing like the quiet period before darkness to bring out the animal life of these places. A doe may walk right through camp or stop and stare curiously for a moment, then suddenly take alarm and bound gracefully away. A golden eagle may perch majestically on a high, bare snag before soaring to his nest. In the northern Montana wilderness there will be glimpses of moose and elk, in South Dakota a herd of buffalo may appear on the horizon or come close enough for their loud snortings to be audible. Stay in your car!

The deserts of the Great Basin offer sights of beautifully marked rattlesnakes, lizards, jackrabbits and many birds. All these creatures are interesting examples of adaptation to an environment. We have seen more blue birds around the old camp of Mineral Park in Arizona than anywhere else, possibly because the many dead trees with deep knotholes provide them good nesting places. The trees and wild flowers to be seen off the beaten track are well worth studying and many a ghost town hunter carries along his botany and wild flower guide books.

I would like to stress the caution we take in making local inquiry before attempting some questionable road. Many of the camps pictured in the Ghost Town books were "secured" by walking to them rather than risk our car on some rutted, steep or muddy road. The maps Dr. Mason has made and included in the books are meant to place the objective in relation to other and better known places on the highway map, not only for armchair travelers but for those actually intending to go there. In fact one really needs our diagram in connection with printed maps. The oldest highway map obtainable is more likely to show the town in question if it is not active now, and the newest map will have the latest highway numbers to correspond with those on the roadside signs.

Our local inquiries have generally been rewarded with reliable information as far as roads are concerned, but the answer to the question—"Is there anything up there?" may leave something to be desired. The answer may be—"No, nothing but a few old shacks." Another person, more discerning, may reply enthusiastically—"Oh, don't miss it. There are all kinds of interesting things up there." And even if the query gets a disappointing answer, if the road seems passable and the distance not too great, it will generally pay the searcher to go and see for himself.

After asking—"What's up there?" and "How's the road?" a third question may hit pay dirt. "Are there any other old deserted towns around here?" It is discouraging to get home after a five thousand mile trip only to discover some gem of a ghost town lies moldering only a few miles from the one you photographed.

Any hobby is more enjoyable when shared by others, so we say to all of you planning to search out some of these fascinating relics of another era—"Good hunting!"

ACKNOWLEDGEMENT
and
BIBLIOGRAPHY

My sincere thanks are given here to the many librarians who have so kindly selected helpful material for study and possible use in the Ghost Town series, and to a long list of individuals who have aided in giving information and loaning pictures of old towns hidden away out of our knowledge.

Suggested Reading

GULCH OF GOLD, *Caroline Bancroft*

THE LAST CHANCE, *John Myers*

THE SPIRIT OF ANN ELLIS, *Ann Matlack*

MONEY MOUNTAIN, *Marshall Sprague*

GHOST TOWNS OF COLORADO, *The American Guide Series*

THE BONANZA TRAIL, *Muriel Sibell Wolle*

STAMPEDE TO TIMBERLINE, *Muriel Sibell Wolle*

COLORADO, *Frank Fosset*

HERE THEY DUG THE GOLD, *George F. Willison*

GHOSTS OF THE GLORY TRAIL, *Nell Murbarger*

OLD TIMERS' TALK, *Ted Raynor*

NO LIFE FOR A LADY, *Agnes Morley Cleveland*

THE PINOS ALTOS STORY, *Dorothy Watson*

ANYBODY'S GOLD, *Joseph Henry Jackson*

BAKER COUNTY SKETCHBOOK, *Gordon and Patricia Stewart*

THE GUIDES TO EACH OF THE WESTERN STATES, *American Guide Series*

THE STORIES OF THE OLD CAMPS IN NEW MEXICO,
                              each by Fr. Stanley, Pantex, Texas

MOTHER LODE ALBUM, *Otheto Weston*

GEOLOGIC GUIDE BOOK OF THE MOTHER LODE COUNTRY,
                              California Division of Mines

THE GHOST TOWNS OF CALIFORNIA, *Remi Nadeau*

OREGON GEOGRAPHIC NAMES, *Lewis A. McArthur*

THE GHOST TOWNS OF WYOMING, *Pence and Hosmer*

COLLECTED MATERIAL ON THE SALMON CITY, IDAHO AREA, *Ralph Irvin*

HERE ROLLED THE COVERED WAGONS, *Albert and Jane Salisbury*

HISTORIC SPOTS IN CALIFORNIA, *Hoover and Rensch*

PHOTOGRAPHY

The first volume of the Ghost Town trilogy raised many questions as to what camera was used, apertures, speed, type of film, etc. Although by far the most frequently asked question is—"What camera did you use?"—I feel that other factors bear more heavily on a sharp "clear" result, such as the consistent use of a tripod. As to cameras, most of the black and white pictures were made with a Rolleiflex using an f 2.8 lens. A sidelight on lens speed is that of thousands of pictures taken with this old "work horse" only one took advantage of such a comparatively rapid lens. This was a hand-held shot of an old couple in their living room, the only available light coming from a window.

A second 2¼ x 2¼ camera, a Soligor, is called upon now and then. It is fitted with a telephoto lens which has several applications. If the photographer can back away far enough (without falling over a cliff or bumping into a prickly cactus) he can pull together several scattered buildings which would appear far apart in a view of normal focal length.

Film for these cameras is usually Verichrome Pan, sometimes Tri X, depending on light conditions in the area or season. All exposures are made with the camera firmly set on a sturdy tripod, taking advantage of the delayed action shutter afforded by the Rollei. This allows the camera to settle down after the shutter release is touched by the finger. I think this one factor has more to do with a sharp picture than any other. Assuming the camera is accurately focused, flared results are caused by movement either in camera or subject. Most of my exposures are slow, 1/2 or 1/5 second, but I believe even speeds of 1/25 or 1/50 are likely to show any movement.

A filter is a must if we are to show proper rendition of color when reduced to black and white, to show clouds when they are present and to help bring out texture especially in wood that is weathered or in reddish tones. Most effective is the red filter, an "A," for example. An orange "G" or yellow "K" is useful also.

The second most frequently asked question is—"What exposure did a certain photograph require?" Some book reviewers have wondered why this information was not given and I have noticed several magazines such as Arizona Highways do include such data. My feelings are there is small chance the photographer will find exactly the same light conditions at a given spot when he arrives to take *his* picture. Time of year, time of day and angle at which the subject is approached make a difference in exposure as do filter used and aperture chosen. The only practical answer to the exposure question is consistent use of a good exposure meter. In my case this has been a Weston Master 3 and its earlier form, the Master 2.

As to aperture, if most of the objects in the lens are at about the same distance, I often use f 8 or so. But often there are objects in the near foreground, as well as the middle and far distance, and to bring everything as sharp as possible, I wind up with an aperture or lens opening of f 22, focusing on a point somewhat less than halfway out. All things considered, with a large proportion of the pictures, I use an "A" filter, film speed of 80, aperture of f 22 and with bright sunshine prevailing, exposure of 1/5 of a second.

As to finishing the black and white, I use Microdol for developing the film and Dektol for the prints. For publication they are enlarged to 8 x 10 and ferrotyped. For public showings they are brought up to 16 x 20 on "F" surface Medalist, and not ferrotyped, then dry mounted. During enlargement considerable "control" is used, to hold back skies or burn them in, to retard exposure of a shaded area in the picture or to increase detail in an over-illuminated section, which otherwise would show only on white paper.

Color slides for public showings, have been done with an Exacta. An eye-level prism finder is generally used for buildings and scenes, while the vertical-viewing finder is easier for small objects, saving a lot of bellywork. The use of two Exactas, and leaving the finders on saves much switching, and avoids much reloading, always an exasperation when picture taking calls for fast action. Tele-photo lenses of several different focal lengths are interchangeable with the regular lenses on the Exactas. Here, as with fast lenses, the expensive long focal lenses, such as 400 and 600 mm telephotos are very seldom needed and for several years have been left at home. A moderate 135 mm and 250 mm are much more useful.

I do not feel a tripod is so essential for color work done with a 35 mm camera, such as the Exacta. Modern color film is quite rapid, the speed is not decreased by filters and the increased depth of field allows more latitude in focusing. Therefore I often leave the Rollei on the tripod and after each picture taken with it, make a color shot with the Exacta, hand held, usually at 1/100 of a second.

All important is the way the light falls on the subject. When the sun shines on an old wooden headboard from the side, any lettering that may remain is brought into sharp relief. An even front light flatly illuminating the same subject may show no markings at all. This principle also applies to old whipsawed boards on the sides of buildings, their edges curling from long exposure to rain and sun. Weathered grain of wood shows up in a side light. Victorian "gingerbread" on old barge-boards likewise shows its intricate, delicate beauty under these light conditions.

Some subjects seem to look fine when shot from the conventional tripod or eye-level height, but experiment will show that others are improved by the photographer's climbing up on an old stone wall or even lying prone on the ground for his picture.

I am often asked if it isn't wise to keep a sharp lookout for rattlesnakes in the desert areas when making pictures. The only answer I have is for me. I don't bother them and they don't bother me. I regard them as interesting types of wild life, to be studied and respected but not feared when encountered.

ALPHABETICAL
Table of Contents

"You feel it . . . yet there's nothing to touch!"

CRIPPLE CREEK, COLORADO

Bob Womack's first trip to Colorado was not a success. In fact, the whole idea was so repugnant to him that he ran out on his father and started the long journey back to Kentucky walking barefoot. After walking more than a month and reaching a point somewhere in Kansas, he was overtaken by the elder Womack, Sam, and the two returned home together.

Sam had taken the boy to Idaho Springs in the famous gold country around Central City in 1861 for two reasons. He would remove the seventeen year old Bob from danger of conscription into service in the Civil War by getting out of Kentucky and in going to the wilds of Colorado he most likely would find a big strike.

After this first move, Sam saw that he hadn't laid the proper groundwork, and now he started a program of propaganda, about all the wealth to be made in the gold fields of Colorado. This was so successful that the whole Womack family was bitten by the bug, and soon all six of them set out for Idaho Springs.

Here the male members of the family, the two boys and the father went to work in earnest, learning all they could about mining. This must have been considerable, because they piled up some money. With this and experience gained, they worked a claim of their own, a piece of ground that had a rich vein of silver in it. It was in the area that later became Georgetown, and some time af-

ter the tenure of the Womacks, yielded a bonanza of half a million dollars.

Sam and his family did not get in on this kind of money, because he had decided his health could no longer stand mining, and would benefit by a stint of cattle ranching. There was enough cash with which to buy a cattle ranch in the wild area south of Pike's Peak near Mount Pisgah. And this move turned the wheels of destiny for the gold discovery that was to yield more wealth than any other area on earth up to 1930—well over $400 million in gold. Cripple Creek. And how was the spot so named? One of the streams draining the area originated in a spring near the cabin of a cattleman, the first settler. While he was building a shelter over it a helper accidentally discharged a gun, the ball wounding another man in the foot. The commotion frightened a calf which broke its leg jumping over the creek—all of which caused the rancher to exclaim: "Well, this here is sure one hell of a cripple creek!"

Bob Womack wasn't cut out to be a cattle rancher, or farmer of any kind; in fact the only career he was really suited for was drinking himself into one stupor after another, and this he proceeded to do. But there were lucid intervals of devotion to a fanatical belief that a rich lode of gold lay beneath the Mt. Pisgah area, particularly in the ground near the cabin he had bought in what he called Poverty Gulch.

MINING MAGNATE'S HOME. Most mine owners of Cripple Creek had elaborate homes in more elegant Colorado Springs but some built houses close to "diggings" in earlier days when actual presence at scene of operations was still demanded.

There was no logical basis for Bob's belief. The terrain didn't have the right type of rock and every geological formation was all wrong and the experts in nearby Colorado Springs all concurred that Bob Womack was crazy, drunkenly crazy. If Bob had left the country he himself might eventually have come to that conclusion but he stayed on—and one day found a piece of rock which assayed $200 per ton. This was in 1878 and the find should have set off a boom. It didn't because no one would believe anything Bob said or did, even with the piece of rock as evidence. This was due partly to his carousing, partly to painful memories of a huge hoax perpetrated by one "Chicken Bill" and called the "Mt. Pisgah Hoax" through an error in locale. The spurious "discovery" had been made at Mt. MacIn-

tyre and had produced "ore assaying $2,000 to the ton." There was a frantic rush to the spot, then a complete deflation as the thousands found they had been hoodwinked.

But an angel was brushing Bob Womack's shoulder. A comparative newcomer to Colorado Springs, a dentist named Grannis, borrowed $500 and invested it in the man who thought no more of a bottle of whiskey than he did his right arm.

Grannis had gone into the geology of the ground on the slopes of Mt. Pisgah with an open mind and came to the conclusion that Bob could be right, that this spot was the center of an ancient volcano and had the type of conformation that should show vertical plugs, or gold-bearing veins, especially in view of the regular findings of "float" pieces con-

16

taining gold that must have broken off from such hard outcroppings.

This reasoning proved to be right and so was Bob Womack. In 1890, after using up a large part of the partnership money on whiskey, he got a little digging equipment and uncovered the top of a rich vein concealed by several feet of cow pasture. But Womack's reputation was always ahead of him. Even though the partners took samples into The Springs and displayed them to all and sundry, nobody cared to do anything about it. After all, wasn't Bob Womack a blowhard? And what about that other hoax?

About this time, James Pourtales of Colorado Springs, a German count and a man of immense social prestige, decided to take a fling at a claim not far from "The El Paso" which happened to be the claim of Bob Womack and Dr. Grannis. He had no trouble interesting big money and soon things were buzzing all over the area, miners as thick as fleas and all claims paying off. Shacks were mixed in with tents and two-story false fronts with no semblance of order, foot traffic and wagons made their way in every direction through mud or dust.

Horace Bennett and Julius Meyers were partners who had bought up a good deal of Cripple Creek land as a cattle range before the gold fever took over. In 1891 they decided to lay out a town, bringing order into all this chaos, and, incidentally make a tidy pile of cash selling lots at the same time. November 6th the new town was laid out on paper in Denver. When the plan was transferred to the actual site, the planners were only a little dismayed to find that the map didn't lay flat on the actual ground, which was all up and down in every direction, with the steepest pitch from high on the north to low in the creek bed on the south. The main east-west streets were, of course, named Bennett and Meyers and the crossing north-south ones were numbered. Bennett Avenue was the main thoroughfare from the start, and soon filled with every kind of business structure, from schools to red-light houses.

Later, the places of less repute were moved over to Meyers Avenue. That street became solidly lined with at least 70 saloons, uncounted large brothels and even more numerous individual cribs. These were placed strictly in order of preference, starting with young white girls at the upper level, ending up with the cheaper, older women and minority groups at the bottom of the hill, near the trestle.

Near these hook shops on Meyers Avenue were many cheap rooming houses and dance halls, their situations and uses often overlapping, and one of these was the Central Dance Palace. On the upper floor were rooms and in one of these started the first big fire in the town. A gambler and his woman, Jeannie Larue, lived here, but not in peace and harmony. One of their more violent fights ended in the overturning of the gasoline stove. In moments the whistle of the Mocking Bird Mine was

CRIPPLE CREEK, SANGRE DE CRISTO RANGE and Rockies in distance. Competing, adjoining townsites, laid out in '91 and '92, were Fremont (for the explorer) and Hayden Placer, just above. Both names and separate identities persisted for a time, but both became "Cripple Creek" shortly. Plans made on paper sagged and humped on ground, one result was split level of part of Bennett Avenue. Old joke—"I hear someone fell off Bennett Avenue last night and broke his leg"—had some basis in fact.

MAIN STREETS OF CRIPPLE CREEK are Bennett Avenue and Meyers Avenue, run east and west, right to left in picture. Catholic Church and Hospital are large buildings at top of first hill. Most other brick structures are along Bennett Avenue. Meyers Avenue, one block south and parallel, was lined mostly by more frail, cheaper houses of extensive honky-tonk lane. These included the establishments of such famous Madames as Mother Duffy, Lola Livingstone, Hazel Vernon and Ellen Holden. These, along with cribs for individual girls and innumerable saloons and dance halls, have largely succumbed to old age and fire, though enough remain to attract the tourists.

shrieking one blast after another. This was the signal that a major fire was burning, calling out volunteer firemen to fight the flames. This one was bad enough, but a few days later a worse conflagration almost destroyed Cripple Creek, and left most of the residents homeless, hungry and freezing. Satellite towns, bitter rivals in normal times, rose to the emergency in a crisis and rushed food, blankets and tents to their neighbors.

This happened in 1896. It marked the end of the era of flimsy wooden structures to a large degree. Buildings constructed to replace those destroyed by fire, were mostly of brick, changing the face of the town.

By 1889 the mines had produced $21,000,000, and in 1900 the year's production was $23,000,000. During these prosperous times several railroads served the city, and the towns in the district were connected by a network of electric trains. 1894 and 1903 saw dark and violent periods brought on by labor disputes, the worst ever suffered by any mining community. Many murders, the blasting of properties by dynamite and other desperate acts of sabotage came to a head in the blowing up of the railway station at Independence, killing a number of men, maiming and injuring many. This act broke the back of the Union, as public reaction brought squads of soldiers and guards to jail many of the agitators and quell further disturbances. 112 men involved in atrocities were deported to Kansas and New Mexico, but these states did not welcome them, and forced many back.

By July, 1904, peace had descended, but other troubles were besetting Cripple Creek and the nearby towns. Water was becoming an increasing menace in the deeper mines, flooding equipment and preventing operation. Many of the older properties were petering out, and it was becoming apparent that the gold in Cripple was not inexhaustible.

Huge projects of tunneling through the granite walls of the bowl constituting the district were undertaken. Water levels dropped and mining was resumed at the lower levels.

Bob Womack died penniless in Colorado Springs on August 10, 1909. He had reached the age of 66 in spite of his heavy drinking, but his last years had been ones of poor health and poverty, as contrasted to the fame and fortune that came to so many of his contemporaries. Cripple Creek's gold had made thirty millionaires, and most of them did not stop at just one million. Winfield Scott Stratton, for example, who had earned three dollars a day before he began his career in the mines at Cripple at forty-four years of age, left over $6,000,000 when he died and this was only a small part of his take, his endowments, gifts and charities amounting to several times this sum.

Production of gold in Cripple Creek in 1903 was $19,000,000. This was $6,000,000 off that of the year before, and the trend was set, continuing until the present time, when all big operations but one, The Carlton Mill and Mine, have ceased.

The place is not dead. There are too many buildings, old mines and other sights reminiscent of Cripple's history for the tourist to see. The roads from Florissant and Colorado Springs, while spectacularly laid out through the mountains, are perfectly safe and the scenery alone makes the visit well worth while.

The Wall Street Journal of December 4th, 1961, reported: "Cripple Creek, Colorado—Golden Cycle Corp. will quit processing gold ore in its Carlton mill here. The plant will be closed and put on a stand-by basis Dec. 31." The president, Merrill E. Shoup, blamed the demise of this plant, which had operated for more than 70 years, on the low price of gold, stating the mill and mines had been kept going at a loss the past three years.

VICTOR, COLORADO

Victor was never reconciled to being called a suburb of Cripple Creek but its history is so tied up with that of its larger neighbor that it is a component part. Physically connecting the two is a road partly paved with gold ore just a little too low in assay value to be profitably refined when there was such an abundance of richer stuff.

The earliest mines in the neighborhood of Victor included the "Victor" itself and were located in 1891 and '92, but at first there was no thought of a town on the site. When one began to grow there in haphazard fashion a couple of brothers, shrewd promoters, saw the possibilities of getting in on the ground floor.

The Woods boys were looked upon as "Pillars of the Church," "Founding Fathers of Victor" or scoundrels, depending entirely on the viewpoint. It appears they never overlooked the possibility of a "fast buck" in any kind of a deal. The two, Frank M. and Harry E. were deliberately launched on their career by their father, Warren Woods of Denver with a cash advance of some $10,000. The boys first built a reputation for being pious, upright citizens and supporters of the Baptist Church, the Y.M.C.A. and other religious and civic activities. Once the background was established they lost no time setting up a real estate operation on the site for which they had paid $1,000. The location was the Mount Rose Placer which had belonged to a Mr. McKinney and it comprised some 136 acres. The new town was named Victor, after an early homesteader in the area, Victor C. Adams. The brothers advertised that every Victor lot was a gold mine. Now this statement was a strictly promotional gimmick, and not necessarily meant to have the ring of truth. But as the plat was developed it turned out that the blurb was literally true. Not too long after the place got going, an item appeared in the Denver Republican of January 1, 1889 which said "Here you find mining operations carried on in backyards. Gallows frames rearing their heads away above the roofs of houses, thundering giant underground detonations which shake the floor on which you stand and the constant rumble of heavily laden ore wagons through the streets, alleys and vacant lots each seeking the shortest way to the railroad."

As a real estate promotion the laying out of Victor was a fantastic success, but was nothing compared to the profits that poured into the coffers of the Woods boys when they decided to start a hotel,

the Victor. The hotel itself was only incidental. Frank Woods was overseeing the grading operations where the hostelry was to rise when he noticed a gleam of yellow in the dirt. Watching closely he saw the streak widen to an eighteen inch vein definitely auriferous. Frank was one to keep his silence, and even the workmen on the scene didn't suspect what was transpiring. Woods decided the vein was an offshoot of the "Gold Coin," a modestly rewarding mine nearby. He bought the property for a few thousand dollars. Less than a year later his Gold Coin was turning out $50,000 every month for the Woods. Flushed with success, Frank built a brick shafthouse with stained glass windows over the mine.

Shortly after this development other mines were found nearby and even within the city limits. These

ORNATE DECORATIONS BEAUTIFULLY PRESERVED.
Building is isolated by past fires, was near home of old Victor Record on Cross Street. Paper was said to be mouthpiece of W. F. M. During Union troubles militiamen invaded offices to haul off editor George Kymer and four employees. Beautiful linotypist named Emma Langdon, the "Barbara Frietchie of Victor," barricaded her door and spent the night setting up paper which appeared in morning carrying banner head reading "Somewhat disfigured but still in the ring!"

FIRST CHURCH OF CHRIST, SCIENTIST crumbles on steep side street of Victor. During boom days town had several churches. Victor Daily Record of March 16, 1905 ran story stating, "The gospel pursued in hot haste the immigration of the people. In those days the Masons, Elks, Odd Fellows, the Unions and Churches would hold meetings in the same humble structure but on different nights . . . obstacles to religion were work . . . the never ending toil on the Sabbath."

included the Portland, Independence, and Strong. The city became covered by claims, many being worked under the streets and buildings. Fortunately the supporting rock was of an obdurate nature, preventing structures from "falling in." As more mines were discovered and developed the economy of Victor began to approach that of Cripple Creek. Then Cripple Creek suffered its most disastrous fire.

In a time like this rivalry was temporarily forgotten. The morning after the fire, Cripple Creek found itself flooded with food and blankets sent over from a sympathizing Victor. And when Victor, in turn was leveled by a mighty blaze, which started in Jennie Thompson's "999" dance hall, it was substantially aided by its big sister. In more normal times there was plenty of back biting; snide allusions were constantly seen in the press and as usual the smaller contender was the more bitter. The Semi-Centennial Celebration was held at Salt Lake City in July of '97. In the parade was a float sponsored by Victor, Cripple having none.

Comment on the situation in the Victor Daily Record was "Victor did the nice thing by Cripple Creek when our representative at Salt Lake invited Miss Gully, the Cripple Creek Queen to ride on the Victor float. We might say that Cripple Creek took a ride on Victor's band wagon, but Cripple has often done that in the past and the habit is growing." And again, when Independence Day had fallen on a Sunday and Victor had celebrated regardless, the Record commented on Cripple's criticism, "The Goody Goody people of Cripple Creek mean to suppress all sorts of patriotic doings on the Fourth, (Sunday). Patriotism must be below par with our neighbors for didn't they close up gambling on Friday and reopen the games on the following Sabbath? Is it more a desecration of the Sabbath to have a drilling match than to go on a Meyers Avenue debauch? Is it worse to play baseball than faro or roulette? Oh, consistency, thy keepers are not the divines of Cripple."

During the big days of Victor the town was

served by five railroads. One of them, the Cripple Creek Short Line from Colorado Springs cost its owners $5,000,000 and was completed in 1901. Theodore Roosevelt visited Victor that year, riding on the Short Line. The scenery along the way, he said, "bankrupts the English language." All operations of mines and trams were electrified and a highly complex system of electric trolleys was woven around the camp. The Colorado Mining Resources in 1904 said that the district is the only one "in the world where the miner can go to work in an electric car, descend to the mine in an electric hoist, do his work by electric light, run drills operated by electric air compressors and fire his shots by electricity, from a switchboard remote from the point of explosion."

So much "blossom rock" was encountered in the workings that many miners were tempted beyond their strength and indulged in highgrading. The practice became so general that a society for the purpose of protecting the miners involved was organized, the "Highgraders Association." Exchanges were organized for the purpose of receiving the rich material, but internal disorders developed as miners accused the operators of keeping more than their share of the profits, and several offices were bombed. At least one of the dynamitings was blamed on mine owners who were understandably opposed to the whole thing. Overall losses from the practice of highgrading were tremendous, one mine alone, the Independence, losing $1,000,000. Many measures for prevention were attempted, none being entirely effective. At the Independence the men were for a time compelled to strip naked at the end of each shift and pass inspection. This stringent order was later rescinded and a milder one substituted—the men could keep their underwear on. One can't help wondering whether the rigorous winter climate might not have had something to do with the modification.

The Woods brothers found shortly after the turn of the century that they had overextended their empire without seeing to it that competition was stymied. Troubles compounded troubles. The hardest blow and the beginning of the end for them came in 1908. They had been busy for several years forming a huge combine of more than a hundred Cripple Creek District mines called the United Gold Mines Company. At the same time an autocratic, driving little man from St. Louis, where he had amassed several millions out of his genius for chemistry, appeared in the district. His name was John T. Milliken. He built the Golden Cycle Mill at Colorado City and it was so successful that in

five years it had driven the Guggenheim mills out of business. Catching the Woods brothers in a shaky period, Milliken bought their United Gold Mines Company at a bargain price.

The Woods' financial disaster was only one of a series that now threatened their whole empire. Among other mistakes made, was that of entering the electric street car business in Pueblo, Colorado. The Thatcher family there, firmly entrenched in Pueblo's business since Territorial days, made short work of the Woods' intrusion by seeing to it that some of the brothers' creditors foreclosed on them. Added to this was the ruin of the Hydroelectric Power Company street cars which were to have been a main outlet. In 1910 the Woods Investment Co. was defunct and the brothers moved away. Harry died with small resources in Laguna Beach, California in 1928. Frank lived until '32, dying in Los Angeles so destitute that a collection was taken up for his burial.

STATELY CITY HALL displays old fire equipment. Ever-present menace of fire in severe winters took heavy toll of mining camps. Victor fire of 1899 destroyed business section from First to Fifth Streets and from Portland Avenue to Granite Avenue. It took out two railroad stations, the elegant Gold Coin Shaft House and the Gold Coin Club. Woods boys lost dozen properties, rebuilt immediately, on credit, more lavishly than before. Fire started in "999" Dance Hall. Other palaces of joy were named Bucket of Blood, Crapper Jack's, Great View, Iron Clad, Rose Gordon's, The Red Onion, Red Light.

COLORADO

LAKE CITY, COLORADO

Only a little moonlight entered the house in Lake City that night in April, 1882. Sheriff E. N. Campbell and his deputies waited silently for the pair of saloon keepers who had been robbing the house of its furniture and were expected to return for more loot. Campbell and his men were beginning to grow stiff and cramped when a noise at the door galvanized them to attention. The sheriff called out, "Throw up your hands!" Instead, the intruders fired at the dimly seen shapes, killing Campbell. They then fled in the darkness.

At daybreak next morning a pursuing posse on horseback caught up with the fugitives who were tied up, taken back to Lake City and thrown into jail. Saloons were closed by the Mayor. Dance halls and stores voluntarily shut their doors. A heavy cloud of foreboding hung over the mining camp in the mountains.

That evening men watched as the moon dropped toward the mountain rim and as it set, they began moving toward the jail. "A heavily disguised figure," it is recorded, "carried under his arms the ropes; another bore a heavy sledge hammer; others carried rifles and shotguns . . . a hundred or more unmasked citizens were waiting at the jail . . . then followed the dull thud of the sledge hammer against the strong jail lock . . . the prisoners were

marched to the bridge . . . a rope was thrown over a crossbeam and in less than a minute the men were swinging . . . It was one o'clock. The dark shadows were now creeping up the side of the western wall of the little city. . . The falls under the bridge gurgled and splashed mournfully—silence brooded painfully over the great court and jury and witnesses who stood with upturned faces looking at two figures swinging grimly at the end of the rope of Justice."

An oldtimer of Lake City, a child at the time of this gruesome event, told historian-artist Muriel Wolle that just as the moon went beneath the mountain and the men dropped to the ends of the ropes, a great cry went up from the mob, then all was silent. He also recalled the astonishing fact that next morning all the school children of the town were taken down to the creek to view the bodies swinging there. At the conclusion of this educational display, "Coroner Rapp . . . proceeded to the scene, lowered the bodies and summoned a jury who found that Betts and Browning came to their deaths at the hands of unknown parties."

This episode, gruesome enough, was preceded in 1873 by an even more sordid one. A mile above Lake City is a fairly level area, in this land of steep mountains, called Cannibal Plateau. Here were found the bodies of five men, their skulls crushed, the bodies mangled and cut up. Pieces of flesh were missing from each.

The events leading up to the demise of the prospectors and the apprehension of a sixth member are confused, but all stories agree that the men started out on a prospecting trip through the San Juan Mountains in December, 1875. They had originally come from Utah and now were safely holed up in a Ute Indian encampment. With heavy winter snows imminent, the chief, Ouray, urged the men to stay for the winter. Six who refused the proffered hospitality were Packer, Bell, Humphreys, Swan, Noon and Miller. These pushed on into the snowy mountains. Some six weeks later Alfred Packer appeared at the Los Pinos Indian Agency alone. He told a harrowing tale of how his companions had quarreled with each other and, when he tried to keep peace between them, they turned and severely beat him, left him for dead. He said he almost starved but found a few roots to chew on and killed some small game. He requested a drink of whiskey, but didn't seem as hungry as he should, in fact seemed much too well nourished to have subsisted on roots and a rabbit or two all that time.

A short time later he appeared at Saguache and spent considerable money on drink, gambling and women. In the meantime, just after his departure from the agency, an Indian arrived there with strips and pieces of human flesh which he said he had picked up along Packer's trail. The authorities already suspicious, went after Packer and brought him in. There being no jail there he was chained to a rock but escaped.

Early next spring as the snow was melting a photographer for Harper's Weekly was on his way to Lake City. Crossing the plateau above the town he came upon the remains of the erstwhile companions of Packer. The find set off an intensive search for the man, a hunt that was to last for nine years. The miscreant was finally caught in Wyoming and returned to Lake City for trial on a charge of murder. Convicted, he was sentenced to hang, but gained a new trial and this time got off with 40 years. After he had served only a few years he was pardoned. He died a natural death in Denver in 1906.

Members of Fremont's Party of explorers in 1848 had made the first discovery of gold in the valley where Lake City is situated, but had other things on their minds, such as imminent danger of being scalped by the Utes. This same fear of having "too much off the top" caused a long hiatus of white immigration and it wasn't until the Bunot Treaty

BAPTIST CHURCH has survived with little change, bearing new roof and several coats of paint. Cloud shadows on hill make white church stand out sharply from background. Prior to building of churches in mining camp establishing religion was one man affair. Rev. George M. Darley, later pastor of Presbyterian Church (also still standing) conducted services in any place available, even gambling hall or saloon. He once remarked that a pool table made "best kind of altar." He was a humble man of God, being as willing to preach funeral services for one of the "girls" from Hell's Acre or a bandit strung up from a tree as for one of the first citizens of the town.

DENVER AND RIO GRANDE built extension to Lake City in 1889, relieving acute depression of camp caused by overproduction of ores and metals with lack of facilities for shipping. Arrival of rails reopened many mines. During '90s line did flourishing business, two passenger trains a day rolling in from Sapinero, most of population at station to meet them. Town was already long dead as mining center when rails were taken up in 1937. Spectacular trestles, necessitated by rough terrain were taken down, only visible traces now are roadbed beside stream and relic preserved in front of courthouse. Caboose has for company an ore car on tiny section of track.

STONE STRUCTURE DATES FROM EARLY DAYS of Lake City, was built as meeting place and dance hall. Assembly room occupies three-quarters of building at rear, cloak room and entry hall with ticket booth are in front. Large safe and pot bellied heating stove are prominent objects among stored miscellany in "foyer." Swallows nests add to decorations on already ornate cornice. Section of wooden sidewalk, once extending length of town persists here, though nearly rotted away.

Rear of stone building was "service yard," also enclosed were outdoor "conveniences." Stone and weathered wood offer study in varied textures.

of '74 opened up the valley that a wave of prospectors, long pent up, burst upon the area about which had been heard so many rumors of rich gold deposits. Enos Hotchkiss is generally credited with having made the first big strike, his Golden Fleece.

Before long as the boom expanded, smelters, stamp mills and lixiviation works were being built all around the valley. One of the reduction plants was powered by the energy developed from a seventy foot waterfall.

In 1875 Harry M. Woods started a newspaper called the *Silver World*. The sheet was printed in a log cabin roofed with saplings covered with soil. When the editor would walk across the floor or was operating his little press a shower of dirt would sift down.

1876 and '77 were Lake City's best years. The population had grown to 2,500 and there were about 500 buildings. In spite of this metropolitan atmosphere the menace of the Ute was ever present, and had it not been for Chief Ouray's constant rein on his savages the town's position in the San Juans would have been untenable.

The red light section was confined to a small area on Henson Creek known as "Hell's Acre" which included all the elements of the typical early mining camp, the gambling houses, dance halls and those establishments often referred to as "cat houses." This general term identified both organized parlors and individual cribs.

Lake City began to go down a little before the turn of the century when the richest veins began to show signs of depletion, and by 1902 the population had dropped to about 500. There are now many attractions for the tourist, vacationer, fisherman and hunter and they populate the area in summer, living in cabins and camps on magnificent Lake San Cristobal.

"THE PARK OR BASIN in which the city is built," said the Mining Register, Jan. 1, 1881, "is guarded on all sides by mighty walls of mineral which look down upon it from the clouds like giant watchmen." Lake City lies in lower center almost hidden by trees. Road partially e n c l o s e s "Cannibal Plateau" at right, near bottom of grade. Scene is viewed from point b e l o w "Slumgulion Pass," so called because it was camping spot for prospectors who prepared main meal of day there.

CREEDE, COLORADO

"Holy Moses!" was what the man said when he found the rich gold ore and that was what he named the mine. The man's name was Creede and the town was named after him—the town where "Soapy" Smith caught the public fancy and Bob Ford, who had shot Jesse James, came to the same end.

In its lower reaches, where it sprawls out in a shallow trickle most of the year, the Rio Grande is a river famed in songs and stories of the Old West. The stream has another aspect not so well known. In southern Colorado, the Continental Divide, crest of the Rockies, runs east and west for a few miles. Nestled against the northerly buttresses of these snowy peaks is a chain of beautiful mountain lakes where the Rio Grande is born. Flowing east at first, then north about ten miles, it soon makes a sharp bend toward the south. At this point the stream receives the several forks of Willow Creek and near the juncture stands what is left of one of the wildest mining camps of all time—Creede.

Here the Rio Grande is a brawling mountain torrent and Willow Creek no less boisterous though smaller. Prospecting along the banks of these streams in 1889 were Nicholas J. Creede and partner George L. Smith. They had been panning the creek gravels and picking at the rock along the banks all morning. They sat down to eat and Creede, swallowing the last bite, got up to chip off a chunk of rock that attracted him. What he saw on close examination made him stop his wanderings. He had found the ore that was to become "The Holy Moses."

This mine and a second, the Amethyst, found the same summer by Creede, created a boom that had few equals in a state that ate them for breakfast. The first year of the Creede discoveries $6 million had been scratched out of the precipitous rock walls lining Willow Creek. As the motley collection of people from hardworking miners to prostitutes moved in, shelters and stores were hastily thrown together, flimsy from lack of building material and space.

Several canyons debouching onto the slightly wider space where the main part of Creede was built were filled with shanties and hovels crammed against the rocky walls, clinging to them in the clutch of cables or perching precariously on spin-dly stilts. When the melting snow in spring swelled Willow Creek into a raging torrent many of these structures went swirling down to the Rio Grande. Each collection of buildings, separated by a canyon wall or spaced farther up or down the creek, had a special designation—Upper Creede, Sunnyside, Bachelor, Amethyst, Gintown. This last was also called Jimtown and was more or less homogeneous with Amethyst.

The real estate promoters had a flair for fancy names. Windy Gulch became Zephyr Canyon, Mud Flat blossomed out as Meadow Glade. Lots, once acquired at fantastic prices, often had to be defended and several murders were the result of claim jumping. One man wrote home he had asked directions to the "Palace Hotel" and found it a whip-board shanty, 16x16, with a blanket for a door. Beds were packed like cordwood and brought a dollar with covers and "four bits if you had your own," vermin included either way.

Whatever Creede lacked in virtue it offered plenty of ways to go to hell. Every other shack was a hook joint or dance hall, or combination of both, the ones in between gambling houses and saloons. Here and there was a respectable place but if a grocery store it still sold whiskey.

The place was filled with "characters," among them the notorious Soapy Smith. He got attention first by selling a bar of soap "wrapped up in a dollar," the buyer winding up with the soap and not the greenback. Soapy's most spectacular stunt concerned "The Petrified Man." He and his co-frauders made a human figure of concrete and buried it in the wet gravels of Willow Creek. While "the man" was aging the word was passed around that a miner had accidentally discovered this wonder. Soapy then led a selected party to the site, and with all due ceremony exhumed the relic and hauled it to his saloon where he exhibited it, though not for free. At a dollar a head the profits poured in and Soapy saw to it none of the customers got close enough to examine the gruesome object. Then came word of a visit by a famous scientist to inspect this archeological treasure and overnight the "petri-fied man" disappeared, with Soapy's outcry at skull-duggery louder than anyones. Nothing was heard of the concrete "corpse" again.

Bob Ford, who had shot the Missouri desperado

VIEW LOOKING NORTHEAST shows spectacular cliffs bordering Willow Creek. Mines, shaft heads, cribbings, loading chutes once almost entirely covered steep walls. Main mine operation shown here is that of huge Commodore Mine, levels number 3 and 4. Main mineralized zone of Creede region runs just to left of central cliff.

LOADING BUNKER clings to near vertical rock wall. Crusher was operated by electricity, abundant in Creede where it was generated by ample water power. Lights burned day and night all over camp, inspiring poem, "And There Is No Night In Creede."

Jesse James, built a saloon and enjoyed a phenominal business due to his popularity with the sporting crowd. One night when the town was crowded with celebrants at the opening of a new dance hall, a miner named O'Kelly shot and killed Ford. No one knew what the grudge was, even O'Kelly who said Ford had "done dirt" to his parents. Ford's funeral was one of the largest ever seen in these parts with wine, champagne and liquor flowing

"like water." There was hardly a sober soul in Creede that night in June, 1892.

Gold, silver and zinc were among the metals mined in Creede but silver was queen. In fact Creede led all Colorado camps in silver production during its big years. The silver debacle of '93 dealt the death blow and the place was never the same again. There have been several revivals of a sort. In the 1920s some mines were reopened and in 1939 the Emperius Mining Company re-activated the Commodore-Amethyst east of town. Some 500,000 pounds of silver were then shipped out at intervals of several weeks. In a camp with a less glamorous history of big production this would seem phenomenal but it was pin money to this one.

Cy Warman who came to Creede in its roistering days to start a newspaper *The Candle*, left behind a poem which sets the tone not only of Creede, but all the other boisterous camps of that day.

"And There Is No Night In Creede"

Here's a land where all are equal—
    Of high or lowly birth—

A land where men make millions
    Dug from the dreary earth.

Here meek and mild-eyed burros
    On mineral mountains feed.

It's day all day in the daytime,
    And there is no night in Creede.

The cliffs are solid silver,
    With wondrous wealth untold,

And the beds of the running rivers
    Are lined with the purest gold.

While the world is filled with sorrow,
    And hearts must break and bleed—

It's day all day in the daytime,
    And there is no night in Creede.

RAIL FACILITIES were not long in coming to Creede. Grade up Rio Grande was steep but negotiable. Station is situated on small area nearly level, where rest of main part of town was placed. From here Bob Ford's body was shipped back to Missouri after period of burial in Creede. Slayer O'Kelly served term at Canyon City, was released later.

SPAR CITY, COLORADO

Spar City was young and brash with three hundred people. It began as Fisher City with a systematic plan for streets and city blocks in the spring of 1882, going forward "to assume business proportions, buildings going up on both sides of the thoroughfare. A hack line was established between the young town and big sister Creede. That city's famous newspaper, the *Creede Candle*, felt that Spar City was going to have a newspaper and to avoid competition, started a branch— the *Spar City Spark.*

With a fine sense of smugness, this weekly complained about the Indians who were in the habit of camping along Lime Creek and editorialized: "Great indignation is felt, both at the unwarranted wholesale slaughter of game and the neglect of the Agent in allowing the red pests to be away from the reservation."

The first find of float was made prior to 1882 and led to several good outcroppings which became the Big Spar, Fairview and Headlight mines. With this industry behind it, Spar City went blithely ahead with daily mail service and in 1893 confidently predicted it would soon be second in size to Creede. In June of that year silver was demonetized, paralyzing all the silver camps. In the case of Spar City, with no background of any other kind of industry the effect was catastrophic, many people actually suffering from hunger.

Sam Hyde of Spar wrote to the *Creede Candle* that "people living in agricultural regions or large cities may find it difficult to realize how a community of people in this land of plenty can be placed in such a trying position. While a community may have untold wealth at its doors, it is not directly of a nutritive character. A power beyond our control has made our mineral valueless for the time being, our women and the children must be fed, and in short . . . assistance is necessary. Meat and flour we must have."

Creede came to the aid of Spar City with their publicized plan. "Spar is peopled by honest industrious Americans out of work and out of money. They are proud people but they must eat. Having nothing to exchange for bread and meat, they propose the following plan of the New York bankers and issue clearing house certificates backed by their brawn and industry and offer them in exchange for flour." The beef was butchered and sold in exchange for promises to pay when able and flour passed out on the same plan.

In spite of these temporary alleviations the town of Spar City had received a mortal blow. It was gradually bled of its hungry population and barely kept a spark of life until 1905. Then an entirely unlooked for stream of blood was piped in. A group of 150 strongly prohibitionist Kansans bought the town, lock, stock and barrel and made it over for their own uses.

Each summer now sees these people getting settled in their completely made over cabins, preparing to spend their vacations in the magnificent mountain and canyon scenery, fishing and hunting, and "maybe doing a little prospecting."

"DORMITORY" FOR GIRLS from dance halls, brothels and saloons was this, the only two-storied building in Spar City. Porch originally extended length of big cabin, with roof where little balcony now is. Large interior sees festivities again, of primmer nature than in bawdier days. One of prohibitionist vacationers found cabin assigned to him had bar along side and mirrors on wall, lost no time altering decor. Bar had been moved from Creede, was one behind which Jesse James was shot by Bob Ford.

BONANZA, COLORADO

Anne Ellis said the road between Bonanza and Sedgwick was a "rare specimen of engineering skill. A vehicle could get over it without upsetting." She was the author of "The Life of an Ordinary Woman" in which she vividly described her life in Bonanza, having "gone up the gulch at six and come down at sixteen."

Once the bed of an inland sea, the San Luis Valley is level, except for occasional rocky upthrusts, islands in those distant times. The silt laid down then makes rich farming soil and it was this fertility which nourished the miners of Bonanza and surrounding camps in the '80s. With an elevation of just under 8,000 feet, the growing season is short.

Near its northern end the San Luis Valley is squeezed closely by the Sangre De Cristo Range on the east and the Cochetopa Hills on the west. In this scenic situation lies the quaint little town of Villa Grove, once the supply center for the mining camp of Bonanza. It was never a big place but it was lively. Its stores offered variety, one sign reading "Fresh Eggs, Rubber Boots, Corsets." Extending from Villa Grove westward and at stretches, almost straight up, is the old road to the camps which have almost disappeared except for Bonanza, itself none too robust. First came Sedgwick and Kerber City, opposite each other on the stream, then Bonanza and above, Exchequerville.

In her book Anne Ellis pictures the Bonanza log cabins, frame buildings and tents, lining the street that followed the creek, the deep snow, mud and dust; miners walking single file on the lower side of the road; strings of burros with panniers packed full, surmounted by bed rolls, drills, picks and shovels; freight teams coming down with ore and going up with supplies; the stage dashing by with its passengers; the "fancy girls" who had their favorite horses to ride up and down the gulch; the saloons where no woman ever went unless she was "fast." The author once tried to peek in, sure there would be "pictures of naked women, shiny glassware and wonderful hanging lamps."

At first the family lived in a one-room cabin, where, in times of heavy snows, they were confined in a welter of drying clothes, socks and heavy, steaming underwear. Every strong gust of wind blew snow through the shack. The next step was into a two-room shanty. It had a canvas ceiling, and moving bulges there showed where the pack rats were running. On one occasion her mother made a successful stab upward with a long meat-fork and blood came dripping down.

When Anne Ellis came to the end of her life in Denver, she was sent back to Bonanza, to rest beneath the aspen trees in the little cemetery on the mesa above the town.

MINERS CABIN IN BONANZA is of sturdy log construction, has endured from days when busy pageant of life in rowdy mining camp passed its door. Some of good mines of day were Rawley, Bonanza, Empress Josephine, latter yielding total $7,000,000. In '70s, population was 1,300, in '90s less than 100. Turn of century saw short revival.

CRESTONE, COLORADO

"Sangre de Cristo!"

The prospectors and settlers of the slopes and valleys under the snow-topped range could easily picture the Spanish explorer, Valverde, in the early morning when the sun suffused the white crests with a golden red glow. Reverently, the legend said, he removed his steel helmet and covered his chest, breathing fervently those words. In honor of Valverde and his discovery, the settlers named the range extending from Salida to Santa Fe, Sangre de Cristo—Blood of Christ.

KING FERDINAND THE SEVENTH OF SPAIN in 1823 rewarded one of his subjects with title of Don Luis Maria Babeza de Vaca and granted him a trifling few hundred thousand of acres of land in new world. Legal ownership of vast area became serious matter when it was found the City of Las Vegas, New Mexico was included. After many maneuvers and shifting of titles, family was deprived of Las Vegas but in return received four hundred thousand acres extending into Colorado. Grant No. 4 comprises 100,000 acres of land mostly fitted for grazing only. Domain is 12 miles square and contains sources of six streams. Gold, silver, lead, copper and iron were found, several towns established— Cottonwood, Spanish, Duncan Pole Creek and Lucky. Grant owners condoned settlement while development was going on, evicted miners when value of metal finds became obvious. Duncan was saved by re-establishing town as Liberty, just over border.

Eight peaks of the noble mountains rise to 14,000 feet and close to the base of them, with the Crestone Needle spiring up to 14,191 feet, the mining camp of Crestone struggled into recognition in the 1880s. The land here was part of the Luis Maria Baca grant, later taken into Colorado by the first territorial governor, William Gilpin.

In 1879 prospectors were pecking at the rocks in these mountains, as along the whole length of the Rockies. Considerable gold was found, a mild boom developed and leveled off, and in 1890 good free-milling gold was found in "gash veins." Before it

32

was discovered these were comparatively shallow, Crestone had been built.

The town took on the shrouds of a ghost but came back to life in '99 when another good vein was uncovered. Having learned no lesson from the earlier fiascos, Crestone again boomed. This time a hotel was built, real estate changed hands overnight and the railroad was extended to the town. The population had reached a new high of 2,000.

Miners were making new strikes in every crack of the Sangre de Cristos and in 1901 the blood count shot up still higher when the exciting strike at the Independent was made. Surely this vein, the miners said, would be a good one. It would yield for years and keep Crestone on the map. But alas, the vein pinched out as the others had and the town lay down in undeniable defeat. Since then only the faintest of heart beats are detected in the shadows of the peaks, and these in the ranchers' houses and vacationers' cars.

ONE OF CRESTONE'S TWO STORES which face each other on main street. General merchandise was offered, including everything from coal oil to corsets. The Pioneer had living quarters above store, with outside covered stairway. Facade was kept up for appearances sake and is well preserved.

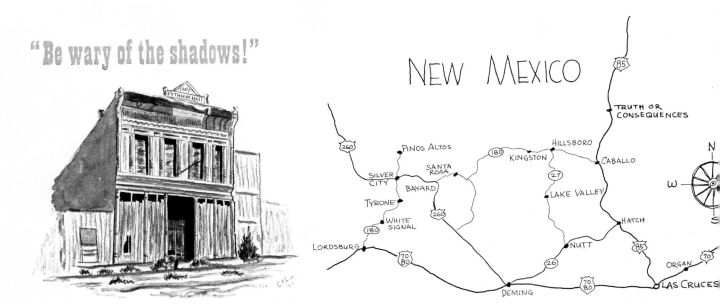

"Be wary of the shadows!"

NEW MEXICO

TYRONE, NEW MEXICO

The unprepared ghost town hunter, arriving in Tyrone, can hardly be blamed if he rubs his eyes in disbelief. Palaces in Spain must have been the models of the dazzling, rococo mansions and public buildings lining both sides of the street in opulent splendor. It is a dusty and deserted street. The ornate arches along shady corridors are crumbling and there are long cracks on the plastered walls of the depot. Patios and pavilions are centered by stone fountains long dry. Where emerald lawns bordered by flower beds once flourished, dry clumps of desert grasses and sage brush now share the courtyards with shriveled corpses of trees and shrubs. Behind these crumbling shells, once so splendid, the hill rises sharply then levels off just enough to give space for an impressive assemblage of imposing Mediterranian-style homes, stuccoed and tiled. Here again are the signs of ruin and crumbling decay, broken windows and fissured walls show that this is no lush resort on the Riviera. Tyrone is indeed unique among deserted towns.

When white men came to the Burro Mountains in the early '70s, they found a marvelous climate, beautiful scenery and Indians busily engaged in the mining of turquoise and copper. Winters in the valleys at the base of 8,035 foot Burro Peak are mild and sunny, summers are warm, there is just enough rain to nourish the typical desert vegetation consisting of juniper, pines, live-oaks and clumps of bear grass. June and July see the magnificent white plumes of "Our Lord's Candles" (yucca radiosa) rising ten or more feet above the valley floor.

But the early whites were interested only in mineral wealth. Their first burrowings were scattered all over the hills, in time became consolidated in larger mines as companies with capital took over. The major operation by 1904 was the Burro Mountain Copper Co. About this time the giant Phelps-Dodge Corporation became interested in the manifestly rich copper deposits in Tyrone and bought an interest in the Burro outfit. Pleased with the results produced under improved methods the Phelps-Dodge people infiltrated the workings until they were the major owners of the whole operation.

There had been two distinct settlements haphazardly growing up near the two main groups of diggings, Leopold and Tyrone. These now became one. Although there were good showings of zinc and lead, they were by-passed in favor of the more available copper. The fact that turquoise existed in the Burro seems to have been kept under wraps —nothing must interfere with King Copper. Ore had been shipped laboriously by wagon and ox team to Silver City where the smelters were, but now a railroad spur was extended from the Deming-Silver City line.

Up until this time Tyrone looked like any other mining camp of that day. The dream of making Tyrone the most beautiful mine town in the world was born in the brain of Mrs. Dodge. The New Tyrone would rise like Phoenix from ashes of the little frame buildings with typical false fronts that had been Tyrone. Her first step was to invite to this New Mexico wilderness the famed architect Bertram Goodhue from his home on the French Riviera. Goodhue also designed the famous buildings of the Panama-Pacific Exposition, San Diego,

STREET SERVED AS "PLAZA" allowing ample space between the buildings as shown in this view through arch of structure across street from mercantile structure centered by three-storied tower and fronted by a facade elaborately ornamented. Building on near side houses once large post office, still operating on small scale for convenience of occasional occupants of houses and for small crew maintained by Phelps-Dodge Co. under same roof.

in 1915. The same fundamental plan was worked out for Tyrone with long arcades along the main boulevard. These were actually covered walkways giving access to stores and public buildings. Mrs. Dodge envisioned a resort town with a large steady population, augmented by a huge influx of tourists in the delightful winters of the valley. The T. S. Parker Hospital was constructed on a rise above the "downtown section," it was amply large and well equipped to take care of several hundred patients. The depot would handle a large volume of traffic and the stores were to carry the largest and most modern line of merchandise to be found anywhere in all New Mexico.

The principal buildings beside the hospital and depot were four large commercial structures, a handsome school with ample capacity, a Catholic church and an office building for the company headquarters. All these structures were planned and built on the grand scale, with no consideration of expense.

A large residential section was laid out on the bluff above the town and filled with handsome homes, many of them imposing two story structures, all in the same old world style. They made a brave and colorful showing in pink, cream, blue, tan and white, each with a tiled roof of red.

More than a million dollars had been spent building the new town and now in 1915 all was ready for occupation. But something was obviously wrong. While a few people bought houses on the

hill and others rented several of them there was no influx. There were alarming rumors being circulated that the rich copper deposits were not so rich as before, and some mines were frankly depleted. Rumors became established facts and no one wanted to move to a failing operation. Added to these calamities was the depression following the war, and in 1921, only six years after Tyrone was completed, the mines closed down and everyone moved away. Everyone, that is, except a skeleton crew in the now shrunken office of the Phelps-Dodge Co.

Tyrone's palatial buildings have been crumbling for more than forty years and have long since ceased to be useful or safe for occupancy. At intervals tiles come tumbling down from the roofs, chunks of masonry or stucco break off from the walls to come crashing down on the paved but cracking walks. Because of the extreme danger, visitors, while welcome to look from the safety of the road, are forbidden access to the buildings. Some of the houses on the heights are occupied by summer vacationers, rentals range from $17.50 per month to a top of $35.00 for the most luxurious homes. There is abundant water and electricity. Tyrone harbors the thought that its ghostly aspect would disappear if it were near a big city.

"PORTALES" — COVERED WALK — ceilinged by exposed beams—"vigas"—runs along entire length of two-story, imposing building planned to house general store, other commercial establishments. Street is at left, view looks toward railway depot.

PINOS ALTOS, NEW MEXICO

In the realm of legend is the story of a long vanished settlement on the site of the present town of Pinos Altos. Prior to known discoveries of gold in 1837 Mexicans were said to have found rich deposits of the metal in a stream at the foot of an enormous cottonwood tree. They erected an enclosure for protection against marauding bands of Indians, the barricade constructed of materials at hand — adobe, stone and logs, built in horseshoe shape. Men and animals were safely quartered inside at night while by day the men placered the gravels, the horses grazing on the hillside close by. In time all their rawhide panniers were filled with treasure and the decision must be made as to who was to take them to distant Chihuahua in Mexico. Here the men fell out. Everyone wanted to stay with the gold and return home. No one wanted to remain at the diggings and guard the stockade.

Here the tale becomes even more gossamer. There would seem to be two outcomes possible. The men all returned to their homes with the golden *chispas* or they fought among themselves and were overpowered by Indians.

Three items in this story are borne out by facts. There were running streams of water even though these flow now only in times of rain. Correlated is the fact that an ample stand of tall pines, *"pinos altos,"* existed before the slopes were wantonly logged off. Gone now is the forest and the streams of clear water once stored by a generous groundcover. Remaining are faint signs of horseshoe shaped ruins, outlined by enduring stones.

More substantial history begins in 1860, when a party of twelve scouts left Tucson for the Rio Grande. A long rest was taken at Mesilla, N. M. Here the men heard rumors, always flying, that there was gold in "them thar hills." Re-routing to Santa Rita they stopped again, this time to stock up on supplies and split into smaller parties. The group made up of three men named Hicks, Snively and Birch made their camp on the banks of Bear Creek and eagerly rushed to begin sifting the gravels of the creek bed. Birch is credited with having been the first to find a couple of nuggets, the *"chispas"* of earlier Mexicans. Frenzied search rewarded each man with a handful of gold. All found it hard to sleep that night and rose early for a council as to what was to be done. The obvious problem was to get provisions and tools if they were to stay

on. But how to keep the discovery a secret? It seemed wisest to go to Santa Rita, confide their secret to trusted friends who would purchase food and supplies so as to rouse no curiosity. The confidants were the Marston brothers and one Langston all of whom swore secrecy. The three discoverers then slipped unobstrusively back to their diggings.

Arising bright and early next morning to begin work, they made another discovery. They were not alone. A party of three Americans had crept in and staked several claims close by. All day and for weeks and months thereafter a motley assemblage of Mexicans, Americans, hard working miners, soft-handed gamblers and con artists streamed in to swell the population of the infant camp called at first Birchville.

The original discovery by Birch had been on May 18 and by September there were 700 men panning the streams. Santa Rita now boomed, supplying staple groceries, as did Mesilla the source for tools and clothing.

At first all gold recovery was done by panning and sluicing in the stream bed, but as rewards grew slimmer, the sources of loose dust and nuggets were found in rich lodes on the hillside. At first these needed only scraping, plenty of ore was easily obtained and crudely refined in primitive "arrastras." A low circular rock wall was built. About twenty feet across, it was centered by a short pole topped by a spike holding the end of a beam that reached outside the wall. A horse or mule, sometimes a burro for small outfits, was tied to the outer end to walk in a circle, dragging a heavy rock around inside the wall. Ore was dumped into the enclosure to be more or less pulverized. At intervals the larger, harder chunks were thrown out and the fine material treated as usual in rockers, Long Toms, sluices, or even in some small operations, panned out.

The town grew to the point where the Mesilla *Times* was running little news items about it. Some of these, gleaned by Dorothy Watson in her *"Pinos Altos Story,"* read: "Thomas J. Marston is pushing ahead his work of grinding quartz, although constantly annoyed by Indians." "The Pinos Altos Hotel serves bread and meals." "Samuel G. and Roy Bean (prominent in Law West of the Pecos) are dealers in merchandise and liquors, and have a fine billiard table." "Thomas Marston wants 200 quartz miners." Marston added that he was willing to pay top wages, up to two dollars a day.

Following this cozy period came a long spell of strife, involvement in the fringes of the Civil War and constant harassment by Apaches. When the Confederacy was established, the area including Pinos Altos was claimed by the South. On August 1st, 1861, Col. John R. Baylor, governor at Mesilla, proclaimed the area to be part of the Territory of Arizona. He then afforded some small protection from Apaches for the settlers and miners by sending Snively, now promoted to captain to help control Cochise's savages, and making another captain of Thomas Birch to watch over his mining camp. About the same time the Apaches made up their minds to get rid of the whites, once and for all. They gathered on September 14, for a concerted attack. Cochise as usual, was in the forefront with his warriors from Chiricahuas, and joined by Mangas Colorado and his band of Mimbrenos, led 400 yelling braves down upon the whites from the forested slopes of the continental divide upon which the camp lay straddled. The attack was begun at dawn and raged until afternoon. The toll of retreating Apaches was fifteen, one of these was killed by a dog belonging to a Mexican miner named Carlos Norero. Two Americans were killed outright and Marston was so severely wounded he died a few days later. He was buried beneath a juniper tree in the little Pinos Altos cemetery.

Although the Indian attack had been successfully repulsed, the miners compared the relative values of gold and their scalps, then decamped in large numbers to engage in what they thought might be the comparative safety of the Army. Some chose the Union side. Others were more in sympathy with the South. The remaining residents felt their numbers were so decimated as to make them targets for further attacks and screamed for help. Governor Baylor responded with a detachment of 100 men under Major E. Waller for their protection.

Even with this another Apache attack occurred in which forty miners were casualties. This one was executed in crafty manner, with a full understanding of the emotions lonely young men must be feeling after such a long time in camp without women. Mangas Colorado stationed a group of his more attractive young squaws on the hillside above the camp in full sight of the miners. The girls languidly combed their hair and otherwise displayed their feminine charms.

At last the men could stand it no longer and most of the shrunken male population made a mad rush up the hill. Apaches ambushed them on both sides and cut off any retreat. Other Indians united and drove off the horses. Additional parties of Apaches seized a number of whites who were hunting game in the hills. One of the hunters who escaped the terrible slaughter reported the hills "full of Indians."

Mangas Colorado had been subjected to many indignities and treacheries by the whites, blaming them as the reason for his continued attacks. General Carlton sent out word that Mangas Colorado must be captured "by any means deemed necessary." Captain Shirland and Jack Swilling located the chief in the Pinos Mountains and conveyed the message to him that the whites were anxious to negotiate and would guarantee his safety if he would accompany them to Fort McLane. In spite of all previous experiences with whites and "negotiations" with them, the chief went willingly and alone with the emissaries. On January 18, 1863, he was shot to death "while trying to escape." With the chief out of the way, the soldiers found courage to "capture" his wife who was taken to Pinos Altos and killed.

The last act of treachery on the part of the whites came in the summer of '64 when a partially successful treaty had established a certain amount of confidence on the part of the Indians, at least enough so that they came peacefully into camp for barter. One of the settlers owned a house larger than the rest. He asked some of the Indians to invite their friends to a sumptuous dinner he would serve them in celebration of the signing of the treaty. Some sixty guests responded. When all were seated the host opened fire on them, killing many, maiming many more. From then on it was not safe for a white to venture out of camp bounds alone or unarmed.

At the end of the war and with the return of most of the men, Indian harassments became less, though were never really absent for any length of time. A Navajo band drove off more than thirty yoke of oxen and were promptly pursued by about fifty men. In the ensuing clash thirteen Navajos were killed and a number taken prisoner.

After the establishment of several military forts in the vicinity in '69, such incidents were replaced by others of a more homely nature. A Sr. Ancheta, resident of Pinos Altos, made a visit to the hacienda of his old friend in Mexico. While there he fell in love with the wife of his host. He talked her into running away with him and as soon as the couple reached Pinos Altos, Ancheta made haste to reinforce the defenses and made port holes in the walls in case the bereft husband should pursue them.

Other men were content to take Indian or Mexican women as common law wives, to build log or adobe homes and start planting garden seeds. Orchards and vineyards were established and except for an occasional murder in the saloons or a miner being killed in a premature mine explosion or attacked by bears while hunting, life in the camp became almost prosaic.

Historian Dorothy Watson paints an idyllic picture of early day Pinos Altos. "They made of their homes a garden spot, there were fields of alfalfa, corn and beans, and smaller plots of garden truck and flowers. Besides his terraced grapevines and fruit trees Mr. Stanley had a rose garden. The Mexicans planted almond and peach trees around their homes and invariably had oleanders in tubs. During the summer they blossomed beside the doorways and somehow room was found for them in their small dwellings when frost came. They took fledgling mocking birds from nests, carefully tended and trained them. They were kept in large cages hanging outside on the walls where they called and exchanged confidences with the neighboring wild birds or complimented the guitar music. Each home had a small corral for a burro. Chickens and cows roamed at will and here and there goats would clamber over walls and roofs. Every day the yard was swept as clean as the mud packed earth floors of their dwellings. Peter Wagnor and John Simon brought wild roses from the canyon and planted hedges of them around their homes. Although the buildings were crude, the effect was pleasing."

The camp flourished for a long period but began to show signs of decay toward the turn of the century. Silver City had in the meantime come into prominence and in 1879 one newspaper there referred to Pinos Altos as "an abandoned camp in Silver City's back yard." The "abandoned" town had a population of 9,000 in the '80s and '90s, boasted a drug store, two hotels, barber shop, clothing stores and even a Turkish bath.

In spite of a downward trend there were several spurts forward, one in 1906 when the long dream of narrow gauge came into camp, enormously expediting the shipment of ores to Silver City. Excursionists were thrilled to ride on the tops of loaded ore cars. On one such trip, returning cars on the steep grade got away, failed to make a sharp turn and landed in the gulch. After this no one but employees was allowed on the cars.

Great excitement was caused in 1911 when Ira Wright and James Bell struck rich deposits in their newly leased Pacific Mines. One lot of 1800 pounds of ore brought them $43,000. As was to be expected this set off a wave of high grading; miners were thought to have taken out as much for themselves as did the owners. All recipients were relieved of temptation when the shallow pocket gave out. Bell and Wright did not renew the lease, marking another downward step in the economy of the town.

During depression days idle men flocked to the diggings, scratching around once-rich shafts and tunnels, trying to eke out a living. Others were operating as many as seventy rockers in the stream beds so that the scene resembled the aspects of early days.

Altogether, The Bureau of Mines estimated, over $8,000,000 in gold, lead, silver and copper were produced in the camp once so blessed with tall pines and streams, now so barren and dry.

GOLD AVENUE METHODIST CHURCH w a s dedicated May 18, 1898. First Pastor was Rev. Henry Van Valkenburgh. Church was built on part of Good Enough Mining claim, the owners donating the site. Methodist ladies gave church suppers, basket socials to raise money for building fund. Phoebe Hurst, member of wealthy mine owner family, offered to help on condition reading room was provided. When edifice was completed it was found that separate room had not been provided, so front of church was stocked with magazines. 1942 picture shows bell surmounting frame tower at right. Earliest church activities were Catholic, diocese was in Mesilla. Priest visited parish, baptized children, blessed casual unions entered into since last visit, said Mass for those who had died.

KINGSTON, NEW MEXICO

A single piece of float exhibited in Denver in 1882, created such a boom in the place where it was found that a whole town was born on the site in a few weeks. The camp was first called Percha City, after Percha Creek, where Jack Sheddon had first found the chunk of rich silver ore. It was surveyed for a town in October of 1882 and by the end of that year 1800 men and some women had moved in. The men consisted of miners and merchants with a sprinkling of gamblers and pimps. The women were mostly the latter's stock in trade, a few others, miners' wives. As the camp settled down to a more steady existence more families became established.

In Kingston's first hectic years, the buildings were of the flimsiest nature, large tents or some combination of fabric and whipsaw lumber. One of the first hotels had walls of canvas and a roof of boards, the cracks in the latter battened to keep most of New Mexico's infrequent rains out. Three tiers of bunks lined the walls. Prices varied, ranging from cheaper shelves above to the more convenient and costly ones below. All patrons were reduced to the same level, however, when frequent shooting scrapes outside sent bullets flying through the fabric walls and everyone dived to the floor and comparative safety. Food served in the kitchen and dining room "annex" came from an outdoor kitchen. Meats on the menu were purchased from the butcher shop near by advertising beef, bear, venison, pork, wild turkey and goat.

At first the camp had no jail, prisoners being tied to a post, gagged if too noisy and at the convenience of whoever was serving as "sheriff," hustled off to the jail in seven-mile-distant Hillsboro. There were no churches for a long time. When the idea of building one occurred a man passed the hat in the saloons and brothels and soon had it filled with nuggets, rings and currency to the tune of $1,500, enough to build a stone structure. One church to 22 saloons was not considered too bad a proportion.

Before the Civil War, the old New Mexican town of Mesilla on the Rio Grande had a little weekly newspaper. The *Mesilla Times* was printed on an old Washington hand press which had been hauled in over hundreds of miles of desert. When that town was captured by Confederates the press was a victim of the general carnage and wound up in the bed of the Rio Grande. There it lay for several years until an itinerant printer who wanted to start a paper in the now flourishing Kingston thought of it. He got help enough to extract the relic from the sands of the river bottom and hauled it to town. Miraculously, it functioned after some repairs and served to get out a crude newspaper and odd job printing for several years. One of the hand bills produced read:

Ho! For the Gold and Silver Mines of New Mexico
Fortune hunters, capitalists and poor men,
Sickly folks, all whose hearts are bowed down;
And ye who would live long and be healthy,
and happy; come to our sunny clime and see
For Yourselves.

About this time Kingston began having Indian troubles. One day the town found itself entirely surrounded by a ring of the dreaded Apaches on horseback, led by notorious Victorio. Unfortunately for the Indians, they had picked a day some miners were ready to go on a hunting expedition to augment the meat supply. Remingtons were handy and loaded, the aborigines were routed in a blaze of rifle fire in a matter of minutes. The defeat caused a long respite in further attacks, but the miners knew that another attempt to sack the camp would sooner or later be made and kept a constant watch. When Victorio and his men did come whooping in and were again repulsed with heavy losses he called the whole thing off, permanently. To show how big they could be, the miners named their newly completed three-story hotel after the vanquished chieftain calling it "The Victorio."

At its height Kingston was well supplied with hotels, with a smaller one and another built later. In addition there were several dance halls, many stores, the Percha Bank, a G.A.R. Post and Masonic, Knights of Pythias and Odd Fellows halls. By this time there were enough families to require a schoolhouse. All these buildings lined up on both sides of the single street above Middle Percha Creek made a fine effect, Kingston was on its way.

"Pretty Sam" had finished a Casino and Dance Hall during this period of prosperity and the whole town was eagerly awaiting the grand opening, since all drinks were to be on the house. The elegant falsefronted building was on the side of the street next to the creek, and as the ground sloped sharply away, only the front was on the level, while the rear of the bistro rested on stilts above the stream. Since this rear section was not finished in time for the festivities, "Pretty Sam" had a man put a few nails in the door leading to a bridge planned for future construction.

Came the big night and the celebration was at its height. Sam had shrewdly set the date on Christmas Eve. An orchestra had been imported from El Paso, the girls from all but one of the various hook joints were dancing and available. The only reason one brothel was not represented was that Big Annie and her Girls from the Orpheum planned to make a big entrance when the party was at its height, and this they did. There was one miner who was not at the party. Drunk, he had forgotten about the opening and had other plans in mind. Banging on the door of the darkened Orpheum he got madder and madder. It suddenly dawned on him where everybody was and he turned and ran all the way to where the glittering casino was swelling to the joints. Bursting in the front door, his guns blazing, he made even more of an entrance than had the Madame and her girls. Big Annie, however, broke for the back door, followed by the rest of the frolickers. The few small nails might had prevented the headlong plunge of Big Annie, buxom though she was, but the pressure from behind was terrific. The Madame was precipitated headlong into Percha Creek, with a few other celebrants to keep her company.

OLD PERCHA BANK stands just below foundations of Show House where Lillian Russell and her troupe once performed. Bank was center of all business in Kingston, transactions were involving sales of mines and claims. Bank furniture, teller's windows are still intact in structure, but all floor space is taken up with storage of mine equipment. Little ore cart has position just inside front door. Bell was used many years to sound fire alarms and announce arrival of mail. Small trees in front of bank are young specimens of ubiquitous "Tree of Heaven." (Ailanthus altissima). This fast growing, self sufficient tree was originally introduced by Chinese miners homesick for some reminder of their homeland. Seeds blow in wind and suckers spread underground, resulting in widespread propagation. Plants are rapid growers, reaching height of twenty feet in three or four years.

HILLSBORO, NEW MEXICO

Dan Dugan was all for throwing it away and forgetting about it so they could get on with future searching. Dave Stitzel said "No" for a time and then seeing it was no use bucking such Irish stubborness, slipped a couple of pieces in his pocket. The partners agreed on most matters but this April day in 1877 they had run across some float on the east side of Black Range and couldn't see eye to eye on its value.

The two moved on. Discouraged over the poor results of this prospecting jaunt, they were traveling in rough circles intending to return to Santa Rita in the Pinos Altos Range. After more half-hearted poking and picking in the Mimbres Mountains, part of the Black Range, they crossed the valley of the Mimbres River where there was a large stamp mill and the usual assay office. Here they were to rest a few days.

Stitzel slipped away, taking his rocks to the assayer. His partner would only have laughed at him. He was prepared for a delay for even though prospectors were first in line at the office, several days were necessary to run an assay. The pieces of ore must first be crushed into pea-gravel size and ground to powder. A measured amount was then roasted, a "button" of metal melted out and weighed, the comparison to the ore sample given in terms of value per ton. Dugan was impatient to be on his way after hearing what his partner had done. When he got the value news he was impatient to go back. The finished assay ran $160.

The men immediately returned to the float site and established a claim. This first one was called the Opportunity, a second one christened Ready Pay. Both were successful, the first five tons of ore bringing the partners $400. Soon others were flocking in and a name for the new camp was needed. Each man wanted to name the place after his home town. When no agreement was reached, a hatful of names was shuffled and Hillsborough drawn. In usage it was shortened to Hillsboro.

Only seven miles from Kingston, another mining camp, the narrow mountain road through Percha Canyon connecting the two was full of hazards. The road itself was dangerously steep and rough, washouts were common and rocks often rolled down on the coaches, but the most feared danger was that of bandits. There were plenty of

MAIN STREET OF HILLSBORO is unchanged from days when Billy the Kid visited saloons and on one occasion ducked into back room when posse was on his trail.

places along the road where stagecoaches had to slow down to get through and robbers chose these spots for surprise holdups.

Large amounts of gold were often shipped to the railroad at Lake Valley, via Hillsboro, and the return trip was likely to bring the payroll for both mountain camps. Every so often road agents would relieve the drivers of their bullion or money and many were the methods devised for circumventing them. One Bill Holt, a driver for the Orchards Line would make a slit in the collar of one of the horses, remove some stuffing and insert the money in the cavity. Bulky bullion was more difficult to conceal but was sometimes saved by having guards raise their weapons at each narrow pass, ready to fire on any holdup men that might be waiting. The killing of two of them discouraged such surprise parties for a while.

Hillsboro is very quiet now. Enough people remain in the town and surrounding countryside to form small congregations in the two churches, Catholic and Protestant, but very little business goes on and most of the buildings are vacant.

SUBSTANTIAL AND COMMODIOUS JAIL, was second to be built in Hillsboro. Original was windowless adobe cell, part of tiny courthouse on main street. This one, built about the same time, 1893, as second courthouse adjoining was erected to take care of flood of drunks, thieves and highwaymen. Latter were constantly holding up the stagecoaches carrying money and gold bullion between Kingston, Hillsboro and Lake Valley, mining towns linked together by common needs. Hoosegow was three weeks' home of Oliver Lee, James Gilliland and William McNutt, in one of most famous murder trials in New Mexico. Prisoners were fed during tenure by Sadie Orchards, retired from stage driving and operating hotel in Hillsboro. Jail is roofless, allowing sun and rain to nourish grass in cells.

MAIN ENTRANCE TO COURTHOUSE, Murder trial for killing of Judge Fountain and his nine-year-old son was held here, although crime supposedly was committed near Las Cruces. Public feeling against the men held for murders was so intense that lynching was feared, and prisoners were moved to Hillsboro under cover of darkness. No trace of missing judge or boy was ever found; for lack of any corpus delicti or evidence of foul play three weeks trial ended in not guilty verdict. Town had been so loaded with curious spectators all hotels were filled and cowboys camped beside their chuck-wagons.

LAKE VALLEY, NEW MEXICO

On the map of New Mexico, Lake Valley lies at the bottom or south end of an inverted L. Kingston is at the other, western end and Hillsboro at the junction. These three towns in the wild and wooly days of the 1880s and '90s composed the stage route of the Orchard Line.

Sadie Orchard knew it well. She ranks among the most colorful characters of New Mexico's early days. She came to the Territory in 1886 and seeing the advantages of having the only stage line in the region, she and her husband assembled two Concord Coaches and an express wagon as a nucleus. She drove one of the coaches, making the full run from Kingston to Hillsboro to Lake Valley. It was her proud boast that her coach had never been held up while she held the reins. This could not be said of the stage line as a whole for bandits and Indians waylaid the stage and freight wagons with discouraging regularity. Sadie is said to have shaken her head about the worst stretch on the route, narrow Percha Canyon. "It sure was troublesome for us stage drivers. Indians lurked along the way and the road was surely trying."

Lake Valley hadn't always been the important terminus of a stage line. In the '70s it was only a tiny settlement and few people knew of it. More did very quickly after the August day in 1878 when cowboy George W. Lufkin rode along the

IN OLD LAKE VALLEY CEMETERY some graves like this one of Sarah Collins are fenced. Those graves without protection from digging coyotes became project of Christian Endeavor. Society raised money to place heavy stone slab cover over graves. C. E. also built fence around entire graveyard, keeping out cattle, other large animals. George Lufkin, first discoverer of silver in camp lies here, died penniless, was buried by county.

MAJOR MORGAN MORGANS, veteran of the Union Army ran rooming house in little false front and "annex." By '96 Lake Valley had lost much of population but remainder felt need of religious influence. Town never had church but ladies organized Christian Endeavor Society, bought rooming house, covered walls with oilcloth, hung up seven kerosene lamps, placed chairs in rows. Annex was furnished for convenience of any preacher who might stay overnight. Ordinarily a leader was chosen from members to conduct each Sunday's services. These were non-sectarian; members included Presbyterians, Methodists, Baptists, Quakers, Mormons and Catholics. Dues were ten cents a month, modest sum realized was augmented by bazaars, basket socials. Society was even able to contribute to famine relief for stricken China, flood victims in Monticello, Sierra County, offered food and lodging to any needy persons traveling through Lake Valley by wagon and team.

edge of Black Range, rifle cradled in one arm and loaded for Apaches, his prospector's pick in the other. At lunch time he stopped under a pinon tree. Among the stones scattered about was a piece of float so interesting he put it in his pocket. Later he had it assayed and was told the value of the sample came out several thousand ounces to the ton. Excited, Lufkin got his friend Chris Watson to join him in partnership and the two relocated the source of the sample. They found the spot but no more float. However they did locate several promising claims, one of them near the town of Lake Valley.

Money dwindled and no good vein was forthcoming. The partners sold out to the Sierra Grande Mining Company, made up of a group of Philadelphia capitalists, receiving $100,000 for the claim. This was a good price considering the prospects. The location actually consisted of several shafts and tunnels; one of the latter had hardly penetrated the side of the hill. A lease was taken on this one by a blacksmith named John Leavitt. Two days after the original finders had sold their claim Leavitt broke through into the most fabulous lode of silver the world has ever known.

It consisted of a hollow in the hillside, a "room" nicknamed the "Bridal Chamber." The cavern had walls of solid horn silver. The total silver removed was 2,500,000 ounces bringing $1.11 an ounce at that time. Before it was all scraped out a spur from the railroad had been extended right into the Bridal Chamber and the rich stuff was shoveled directly into the cars.

Naturally this kind of thing could not be kept a secret, and a rush of prospectors, miners and hangers-on poured into a forty-mile strip along the edge of the Black Range, presided over by Kingston, Hillsboro and Lake Valley.

The Black Range Mining District was officially organized in 1881. Most of the population came that same year, when the Apache troubles were at their peak; no miners cabin or settlers hut was safe from raids by Victorio, or his henchmen, Loco and Nana. In spite of their continuing raids, total production in the period up to 1894 was close to $25,000,000.

One of the smaller towns in the area was Chloride. During the period of intense badgering by Indians, a sentry was kept on constant duty there. Old timers gloried in telling about the time the watch fell to one Schmidt, a German fresh from the old country. He had never handled a rifle but was carefully instructed in its use and reminded that a single shot from the weapon would warn the town that an Apache raid was imminent. About the middle of the night the ominous shot was heard, throwing the camp into the usual panic; women and children were hustled off to the blockhouse built for this purpose. Nothing happened. Pretty soon Schmidt came walking sheepishly into town explaining, "I shot her all right, but I don't mean to do it."

In 1883 Kingston was a hotbed of rustler activity. Organized gangs of cattle thieves became so brazen that they even flaunted their identity to the ranchers they had robbed, as no recourse was possible, short of murder. Ranchers finally appealed to Territorial Governor L. A. Shelton to send a full company of militia, armed to the teeth. The governor ordered Major A. J. Fountain to proceed from Mesilla to the Black Range area. Fountain headed for Kingston with almost his entire battalion, leaving only a skeleton force to guard

the jail at Mesilla. Arriving at Kingston, Fountain found that the ringleaders of the rustlers had fled to Lake Valley. Taking a detail of five men he proceeded toward that town arriving there at five in the morning. He arrested one of the most wanted men without any trouble. This was "Butch" whose real name was William Leland. The other of the desired duo, John Watts, made a run for it, and when cornered lifted his rifle. When he saw that he was outnumbered he put up his hands.

"The two prisoners," Fountain wrote in his report, "were mounted on one horse, unbound. At about 4:30 a.m. after the moon had gone down and before daylight the command arrived at the *cienaga* known as Daly's . . . There I halted the command and ordered the men to dismount and prepare coffee . . . I had the prisoners dismount and asked Watts how he was getting along, he replied 'I want a drink bad'. I told him the men would have coffee in a few minutes. He answered that he didn't want coffee, but whiskey and asked me to allow him to go to a nearby tavern to get some. I told him I could not give him permission and rode off and dismounted."

There was a good deal of confusion while the men were unsaddling the horses and unpacking the mules and in the midst of it someone noticed that the prisoners were hightailing it up the road. The men seized their carbines and fired a volley of shots after them. "I directed Capt. Salazar to take a sufficient detail and follow the fugitives. He took six or seven men and proceeded up the road about 200 yards and came upon the bodies of Watts and Butch lying in the road. They were both dead. I ordered their bodies be covered with loose earth in order to prevent them from being disturbed by coyotes . . . I telephoned Lake Valley the fact of their death with the request that their bodies be sent for."

Eventually the cattle rustling ring was broken up, most of its members fleeing toward the Mexican border. Some were intercepted but most escaped. Thus ended rustling on a big scale in that section of New Mexico.

MOST REMAINING RELICS show a d o b e construction, fronted by whipsawed lumber; this one shows unique combination of adobe and stone. Adobe was not of prefabricated bricks as usual but extension of mortar.

WHITE OAKS, NEW MEXICO

John J. Baxter was a disenchanted '49er. For every one who got rich in Calaveras county and other gold diggings in the Mother Lode, a thousand got only broken picks. Many of them left California for the glitter of other fields and Baxter was one of them, wandering eastward into the territory ruled by the Spanish and Mexican military. He found natives from San Antonio, Luis Lopez, San Marcial, Valverde and Socorro escaping the watchful eye of soldiers from the presidios and searching for gold. And there were rumors that some of them found it.

Baxter was curious and vigilant. He tracked one of the peons down a gulch, part of the shallow canyon running east from a mountain to the arroyo which later would form the western boundary of White Oaks. Having had experience with the rigors of solitary digging, washing and panning, Baxter took into his confidence John H. Wilson and John Winters and proceeded to the spot with whatever primitive equipment they could scrape up without creating too much attention.

They did find gold there—lots of it. What they did not find was water. The camp had to be two and a half miles away where the springs were. There were two flows, generous ones for so dry an area, surrounded by a grove of white oak trees. In the morning after breakfast, the men would set out for work at the diggings taking as much water as possible on the backs of several mules. This they would use as sparingly as possible to wash their pans of gravel. At night the

process was reversed, pay dirt went home with them and was washed where the water was.

Hard work paid off. Even little nuggets turning up to cheer the laborers. News of their find got around and when the summer was nearly over they had a visitor. He offered no information except his name was also Wilson. Some said he was from Arizona, others Texas. Most agreed, judging from his furtive manner, he must have a price on his head and wouldn't tarry long. The miners put him up for the night and fixed him a lunch for the next day.

Instead of going along with them to the gravel bed, the new Wilson set out for a walk up Baxter mountain to survey the country. While resting and eating his lunch he idly chipped off some interesting rock and put it in his pocket. He then took a good look around from his vantage point and returned to camp. At supper time when all were assembled, the chips were displayed. Excitement grew as the more experienced miners confirmed what Wilson had only guessed. The whole group hurriedly took lanterns and retraced Wilson's steps, finding the spot without too much trouble.

Early next day stakes were set out and Wilson was asked how much he wanted for his share. He said that gold was of no use to him, he'd have to go, and whatever the others wanted to give him would be all right. He took the offered $40 in washings, $2 in silver, a pistol and another lunch and was on his way, disappearing from the pages of White Oaks history. The others realized $300,000 apiece not much later when the mine was sold as the Homestake. The original claim returned a total of more than $3,000,000 during its useful life.

The early days of gold discoveries in White Oaks were somewhat frenzied even allowing for the florid style of reporting in the newspapers. The *Albuquerque Journal* for April 6, 1881 touches on some of the finds. "One pocket being found from which in one day there was taken by the men over three hundred dollars. For several weeks thirty dollars was average for each man . . . on March 1 was struck another body of ore with gold visible to the naked eye all through the rock . . . An assay of a piece of ore from the last find, showed no free gold, was made on March 24, resulting $17,000 per ton, flour gold. Surprise to relate, the float from this vein, on the side of the hill and the bottom of the canyon, near where the last gold was found on the last soil being washed from it, shows free gold sticking to it on all sides and on breaking gold appears all through the rock. . . The Old Abe seems to be an immense deposit of gold bearing rock. The deposit is about a hundred feet in width."

The town itself grew up on a flat of about 160 acres beside the stream bed. The founding date was August 15, 1879—a tent city growing up even before saw mills could be built or lumber freighted in over almost non-existent roads. Tents gradually gave way to shacks. The first real house was completed July 17, 1880 and occasioned a big celebration. Population in the camp was then about 800 (it was later to grow to 4,000). The growth was so rapid the burgeoning town was splitting its seams, it couldn't absorb all elements in orderly fashion and some sections acquired cognomens of their own. There was Hide Town where buffalo hunters spread their odoriferous wares for curing and tanning. Hogtown was composed of cantinas, gambling dens, brothels, dance halls and like places where the miner could be parted from his money.

The camp was a fertile breeding ground for newspapers, some of which lasted a while, others got out one or two issues. First to come out was the little sheet modestly titled *The White Oaks Golden Era*. A year later partners Fenn and Morse

EXCHANGE BANK OF WHITE OAKS — l a s t survivor on main avenue. Town had 213 houses in 1885. First President of bank was editor of White Oaks Eagle, John Y. Hewitt, whose crumbling mansion also still stands. One historian calls city "attorney ridden" because of plethora of lawsuits over ownership and profits of cattle, horses and mines. Total list of lawyers is long, those having offices over bank were Hewitt himself, W. C. McDonald, later first Governor of New Mexico under Statehood, and H. B. Ferguson, later delegate to Congress.

planned a new paper, *The White Oaks Scorpion*, but this one never even got going. Then came *The Lincoln County Leader*, *The Old Abe Eagle* and the *New Mexico Interpreter*. Each lasted several years. An ad in the *Interpreter* extolled the qualities of a commodity strange in a rough mining camp—Ah Nues Song Birds, "The best in the country, and his cages the most beautiful. Those desiring a lovely singer should give him a call. His prices are very low."

The water problem was solved by the discovery that the moisture table was only about fifty feet down. For more serious drinking "the cantinas supplied various brands of gutrot at fifty cents although quality stuff was higher. After you drank enough of the putrid liquid that had been mellowed by dead rodents, snakes and birds, the quality stuff tasted like poison."

Then there was the more enterprising drinking establishment which put on stag shows in its enlarged building and booked traveling companies such as the famed "Wallace Sisters." The place was called the Starr, after a popular prospector of that name. Not all troupes made a killing at the new Opera House. Sometimes performers were compelled to remain for further shows to get sufficient funds to move on to Socorro.

The least excuse called for a celebration in White Oaks, and such occasions as Independence Day necessitated a real rip-snorter. The whole town turned out to eat at a table "130 feet long, loaded with all the good things of life." Beer and liquor flowed freely and the usual quarrels flared up, though with not too many casualties.

Outlaws of every description left their mark on the town. Among these were Dave Rudabaugh, Joel Fowler, Jim Greathouse, Toppy Johnson and Billy the Kid, attracted to the camp's larger saloons, better entertainment and fancier women. Tall tales of cattle rustling centered in White Oaks. Those episodes in which Billy the Kid and his pal Rudabaugh were involved are bloody episodes in the history of White Oaks. These two had their hang-out at the livery stable belonging to West and Dedrick; many of their depredations stemmed from there. The Kid's contact man in White Oaks for the sale of stolen horses was a man named Wheeler. He was caught trying to handle too large a job, the disposal of thirty head turned over to him by the Kid and Rudabaugh.

JUNIPER-RINGED SCHOOL is imposing structure, best preserved in town, cost community $10,000. Teacher of earlier, smaller school was Mrs. McCinnis, who took over as principal when more elegant structure was completed.

SILVER TONGUED SALES-MAN made pitch for Singer Sewing Machine during week's stay in White Oaks, left most homes equipped with gadgets. House is built of adobe with annex of hand-adzed timbers with plenty of adobe mortar. Building materials, native to site were used in construction of many structures in camp like bistro where Jose Leal was master of ceremonies. On one occasion when *baille* was in progress there, Jose M. Ribera, full blooded Yaqui Indian crashed party. Guard had been posted at entrance for just such contingencies, attempted to stop Ribera, was succeeding when intruder was reinforced by friend Justo Salas. Indian entered, one shooting six-gun, other brandishing knife. General melee developed, ending with cracked skulls for several participants, death for Leal, Ribera and Salas. Mass funeral was celebrated next day.

Short time later Salcedo, full of White Oaks' special brand of rot-gut threw wild shot at M. Leecher in latter's home. Leecher picked up club, k n o c k e d weapon from attacker's hand, dispatched Salcedo with gun. Rash of killings continued, avoided in such smug items as story in New Mexico Interpreter for June 24, 1887, "There is no more orderly city west of the Allegheny than White Oaks . . . Our Supreme Court, M. H. Bellomy held a session on Wed. and Thurs. White Oaks is too peaceable to make this court a financial success and we hope it may continue."

In 1887 clamor for a railroad grew more intense. The *Interpreter* stated that "White Oaks is bound to be one of the best towns in the Territory. It has the precious metals and immense beds of coal right at its own doors and when the railroad reaches that portion of the country, White Oaks will grow rapidly." In 1888 rumors flew thick and fast, "it is generally understood that the Sante Fe road will . . . push from Socorro to White Oaks . . . The Kansas City, El Paso and Mexican Railway known as the White Oaks Line is being pushed with great vigor."

Property owners were called for a special meeting to allocate land for the anticipated right-of-way and station. Instead of making things easy for the railroad company, however, the town's business men decided that since the road "had to build into the city" they would make a killing and put a stiff price on the property, making no concessions of any kind. To their dismay, rails were laid through Carrizozo instead. Although the local worthies begged the company to come on any terms, it was too late. White Oaks had cut its own throat. The effects of this fiasco were far reaching; the town actually died of disappointment, at least it started downhill then and never came back. Family after family moved away and the remaining ones began to tear down vacated houses for fuel. Whole stretches of store and business buildings became empty and roofs fell in. White Oaks was on its way to becoming the ghost town it is today.

MAGDALENA, NEW MEXICO

Socorro is the town where one turns west for Magdalena and Kelly. The old shipping center isn't dead, though sleepy, and has a plaza authentically Mexican. The church of San Miguel is one of the oldest in the country. The town, during the old, wild days, was the current hangout of Russian Bill. Not actually a killer, Bill only liked to pose as one. He suffered from a compulsion to stay in the public eye and the only way he knew how to do it was to keep up a constant stream of practical jokes. The town's patience grew thin, and by one Christmas Eve, reached the breaking point. The main hotel boasted a card room as well as dining hall, and it was there Bill played his last game of poker. He got drunk, and bragged about his marksmanship, proving how good he was by expertly shooting one finger from the hand of one of the players. The rest of the gamblers grabbed him by the scruff of the neck, read a charge against him of "being a damn nuisance" and hanged him right then and there in the hotel dining room.

Some twenty-seven miles west is the old camp of Magdalena, still having life but showing its age in the many false fronts scattered through the town. Alice Morley Cleaveland in her book "No Life For A Lady" gives a vivid picture of her advent there. "We arrived in Magdalena in February, 1886. The town sprawled in the sun at the foot of Lady Magdalena Mountain, a bare and defiant monolith in the midst of her decently pine-clad sisters. . . Halfway up the mountainside, Lady Magdalena herself gazes into the blue sky resting upon far mountain peaks, her face turned away from the town. . . There is a legend that Lady Magdalena Mountain was a sanctuary respected by the Indians, where fugitives, whether deservedly or not, found refuge from pursuing enemies. The legend did not hold after the pale-face came shooting his way into the land. Many a pursuer fell before his enemies in the streets of Magdalena.

"'Please give us a room that is not directly over the barroom,' my mother stipulated to the hotel-keeper the night we arrived. 'I'm afraid those bullets will come through the floor.' It was years later before Magdalena gathered herself together and made it a misdemeanor to shoot within the city limits."

In the 1880's when Kelly was already a boom town, Magdalena was hardly more than a watering place at Pueblo Springs. There was a station of sorts there as a convenience of the stage line from Socorro to the western part of the Territory. There the cattlemen watered their stock on market drives and cowboys unlimbered their legs while they had the chance. The present town of Magdalena didn't occupy its present situation until '85 or so, when it began to grow into the place where "the lights were repeatedly shot out by ebullient buckaroos." It was then getting its water the hard way, hauling it from Pueblo Springs at a cost of ten cents a barrel. Kelly nourished the place by sending down her miners who wished to carouse but found insufficient space to spread out in the narrow confines of the canyon in which Kelly is cramped. On the plain there was room for saloons and dance halls of generous proportions and these promptly took shape. Other factors contributed to the economy, such as the railhead and the sheep and cattle ranches which sprang up in the surrounding ranges. The railroad's purpose was to serve the booming mining town of Kelly, up the steep canyon from Magdalena. One look at the canyon's grade, however, and the engineers gave up, saying in effect to the "city fathers" of Kelly, "If you want a train, come and get it." And this Kelly did, rolling its ore and bullion down the short but precipitous wagon road to the station.

When Kelly died, so did a large part of Magdalena, that part having to do with the shipping of supplies for a vast area of cattle ranches and sheep ranges, but days of the old reckless shootings on the main street are gone and the town drowses.

PYTHIAN HALL, BUILT IN 1907 at height of Magdalena's development, is one of New Mexico's best examples of architecture of the time. Decorations are ornate but lack gingerbread effect of other structure of period. Tiny building at right once housed newspaper office, served many later purposes. Eyebolts above door seem to indicate one time sign or awning. Magdalena's prosperity depended upon that of Kelly, mining camp two miles up canyon. Before railroad came to Magdalena, Kelly's ores were shipped 29 rough and rocky miles in ox-wagons over Blue Canyon road to Socorro. Closeness of railhead enormously amplified output made practical by easy disposal. Many mines in district had euphonious names, as Ambrosia, Cimmaron, Alhambra, Little Louella, Iron Mask, Legal Tender, reflecting literary, political or practical leanings.

KELLY, NEW MEXICO

The road from Magdalena to Kelly winds steeply up a short canyon and then suddenly becomes a street, narrow and rough, bordered sparsely on both sides by the pitiful remnants of what was once a thriving town of 3,000. Most of these claimed their town was the most orderly in New Mexico. "Gunfighting is out, here. Fights are to be settled with fists, bricks or rocks."

Kelly's beginnings concerned a Civil War soldier marching with the Union Army, he stooped to pick up a rock that interested him. He couldn't conveniently keep it with him, so sent it to a friend, J. S. Hutchason. This friend was so excited about the sample that he immediately went prospecting in the Magdalenas, hoping to find the outcropping from which the float had come. This he never did, not even finding another piece to match the original. But he did stake out a couple of claims, naming them the Graphic and the Juanita.

Hutchason was an industrious man. In addition to blasting out his own ore (oxidized lead-zinc) he built a crude smelter of adobe. He had to ship the resulting lead pigs all the way to Kansas City by oxcart over the Santa Fe trail, but still made enough money to keep going. He sometimes took a little time off and on one occasion was pecking around at the rocks some little distance from the Juanita mine. While studying these interesting specimens he was joined by a friend who had a sawmill nearby, Andy Kelly. Kelly was intrigued but didn't show his interest. When Hutchason returned to work, Kelly staked out a claim to the spot and called it after himself. He worked it for a time, but one year failed to do the legal amount and Hutchason who had kept his eye on the project, stepped in and took over, keeping up the assessment work himself. The ore produced by this mine was carbonates with galena, averaging 50 to 60 per cent of lead, 10 ounces of silver and some copper.

In 1870 miners laid out a townsite, long and narrow in the canyon and named it Kelly for the mine now producing well. In the next period of development, a Col. E. W. Eaton decided to put some money into the mines of Kelly, and leased the Juanita. Almost immediately the more extensive workings ran into a rich vein of silver so good that when the news leaked out, a boom was on its way. Now things happened fast. Hutchason took advantage of the fever and sold his Graphic claim to a firm called Hanson and Dawsey for $30,000, and the Kelly to Gustav Billings

LITTLE MISSION CHURCH of Saint John the Baptist still stands on steep street of Kelly. Once private residence, it was remodeled for church purposes. Mission never had a priest of its own, was attended from Magdalena. Although Kelly is now completely deserted, each feast day of Saint John the Baptist, June 24th, sees little chapel filled with about seventy-five people from all over countryside, gathered to attend Mass.

EXTENSIVE RUINS OF BOARDING HOUSE disintegrates beside quiet street once teeming with activity. Adobe, sun-dried brick, was standard building material in southwest where timber is scarce, stiff clay a l w a y s available. Sometimes adobe was mixed with chopped straw for added strength. Also optional was finishing coat of stucco which could be of mud or plaster. Either way, thick walls p r o v i d e d protection against heat, cold. Indians could not set fire to structures to force evacuation as often happened in case of frame buildings.

for $45,000. To roast his own ore, Billings built a smelter at the edge of nearby Socorro in 1881 and operated it for twelve years. During this period the village in the Magdalena mountain canyon produced most of the lead mined in New Mexico.

Until about 1885 Indian troubles beset the camp. Every so often they would come swooping down the canyon, to be repulsed only at heavy cost. Or they would sneak to the edges of the camp at night, stealing horses and cattle. When at last the railroad reached Magdalena, several cars were kept handy to carry the women and children to safety in Socorro in case of an outbreak.

But Kelly flourished. There was now a Methodist church as well as the original Catholic one, seven saloons, several rooming houses and three stores. The three dance palaces supported a goodly number of "frail sisters," some kept in a regular "house," the more independent ones having individual cribs farther down the canyon. Both hotels kept three shifts going on the same beds, the saloons and dance halls on a "we never close" basis.

Jonas Nelson got a short term lease on the Hardscrabble mine and worked it for all it was worth in the time allotted. When he received a check from the smelter, it was so large he was inspired to throw a party the likes of which Kelly had never seen. He built a platform in front of

the mine workings, ordered a special train from Los Angeles. It was a "surprise package" con-taining such goodies as champagne and beautiful girls. The party cost Nelson every cent he had and he had to go back to the pick and shovel, but he always maintained "It was worth it."

In the '90s, sharp-eyed Cony Brown wondered about the greenish rocks so common everywhere in Kelly and sent some samples for analysis. When the report came back, he took a lease on the old dumps and all available workings not in active operation before he made details of the paper known. He had found the "worthless" green rock to be Smithsonite, zinc carbonate, a rare and valu-able ore. This discovery set off another boom.

In 1904 the Sherwin-Williams Paint Company bought the old Graphic for $150,000 and the Tri-Bullion Smelting and Development Company bought the Kelly from Billings for $200,000, build-ing a smelter on the spot. Zinc recoveries made Kelly the leading producer of that metal, output between 1904 and 1928, $21,667,950.

1931 saw the end of the Smithsonite deposits and a few more years ended the workings of the lead-zinc sulphides. While some of the population held on, refusing to believe the town had died, most moved to other camps, or to Magdalena be-low on the plain. At last even the old die-hards gave up, and today Kelly does not have a living soul to shelter.

"A spiral of gray smoke . . . but there was no fire!"

TOMBSTONE, ARIZONA

Edward L. Schieffelin of Tombstone, Arizona, and Bob Womack of Cripple Creek, Colorado, had several things in common. They were prospectors at heart and each had a stubborn faith in the ultimate riches of his chosen locale. Each did, in time, see his dream fulfilled in a fabulous strike but there the parallel ended. Bob never did do much with his strike because he drank too much and could not interest big money for proper developments of his find. Ed, on the other hand, made the proper contacts right away, kept control of the several companies he formed, and was a prime figure in the development and history of his city.

As prospectors found out, locating a rich vein is one thing, mining it is another. In the case of placer gold, a lot of the stuff may be found loose in the creek bed and may be had for the panning, but hard rock mining is something else, particularly in the case of silver. When Ed made his find he had done his searching all over Oregon, California and Nevada, at last bearing down on a restricted area in southern Arizona, the fringe of hills bordering the San Pedro River. For a long time the search was as fruitless as the others but now he didn't move on. Settling down to a dogged, systematic scrutiny, he went over the ground almost inch by inch. It wasn't easy. Plenty of

WEARY OLD SADDLES in harness house of O. K. Corral bear mute testimony to hard usage in days when chief means of transportation was riding horse. These were used by Wyatt Earp, McLowery brothers, Clantons and others of the day.

O. K. CORRAL supported large blacksmith shop, used several anvils. This one saw service over long period in '70s and '80s. Most of auxiliary tools are intact and in their original places.

rattlesnakes and gila monsters lurked under every other bush but the most dangerous hazards were bands of marauding Apache Indians. This tribe had more tenaciously and vindictively resisted the white man than any other. And, in fact, the stronghold of the head man of all the Apaches, Cochise, was in the Dragoon mountains, only a few miles from the San Pedro.

Ed tried to work the country under the protection of a group of soldier scouts stationed at Fort Huachuca, but felt too restricted, and informed the men he was going to set out on his own. Asked what he was really looking for, he told them that he expected to find something very useful in the valley. Loud laughter greeted this evasive answer and one of the soldiers said, "Sure you will and it'll be your tombstone."

In approved fashion, Ed persisted in looking for "float" and then searching for the lode or vein from which it came. And finally, there it was, a rich vein of silver, close to the hideout of the Apaches in the Dragoons. The grim joke about

OLD CHAINS ARE DRAPED across hitching rail of O.K. Corral Stable. Original building was in bad state of repair few years after famous shooting scrape in yard, was repaired and restored with authentic atmosphere. Visitors can now browse around stable and yard, almost hearing again fusillade of shots.

his tombstone had rankled, likely because it could so easily have materialized, and he felt a deep satisfaction in naming his claim "The Tombstone." With help in the form of his brother, Al, and one Richard Gird, a clever mining man, he located several other silver deposits, among them the Lucky Cuss and the Tough Nut. This last had an erratic breaking of the lode in every direction, due to faulting.

A real problem developed in trying to enclose the best of these in the amount of ground allotted to a claim, 600 by 1500 feet, a "tough nut" to crack. Actually, the first find, the Tombstone, proved to be not so rich as he had hoped, and was soon sold for just enough to get a little capital. Then they sold another one, the Contention for $10,000. This last sale was soon regretted, the Contention

BOXES IN TINY BIRD CAGE THEATER were taken at $25 a night and often for a whole week during popular presentations. Theater made no pretensions at elegance, shows were frankly burlesque of most rowdy type. Girls doubled as performers, waitresses and anything else requested of them. Opened December 26, 1881, it was never empty, was a place where lonely, thirsty miners or tired businessmen could always be comforted. As girls served drinks to patrons during prelude to performance, they sang the bawdy songs of the day, giving the place its name. Stoutly built of adobe it is well preserved and the visitor today can wander around the tiny floor and stage where performers of another day cavorted.

YARD OF O. K. CORRAL. Adobe wall and big swinging gate are much as they were in days of famous fight here, October 27, 1881. Fight climaxed long standing feud between Ike Clanton's cowboys and three Earp brothers. Clanton's gang had been vowing to "get" the Earps and had so annoyed the Marshal and his brothers that he decided to put an end to it once and for all. As the brothers and Doc Holliday headed for O. K. Corral they saw Sheriff Behan trying to keep the peace by asking the Clantons and McLowerys to disarm. When the Marshal and his party got near enough, he added his order, "Boys, throw up your hands, I want you to give up your shooters." At this Frank McLowery drew his weapon but was a split second too slow, was shot just above the waist by Wyatt Earp. This set off a barrage of gunfire. When the smoke cleared away three men were dead and two wounded. Only Doc Holliday escaped unscathed. The *Epitaph*, Tombstone newspaper of the day, reported that, "The shooting created great excitement, and the street was immediately filled with people. Ike Clanton (who had run from the fracas) was captured and taken to jail. The feeling of the better class of citizens is that the Marshal and his posse acted solely in the right in attempting to disarm the cowboys and that it was a case of kill or be killed."

yielding $5,000,000 in the first five years. This gave them a better idea of the value of what they held, and they refused an offer of $150,000 for the others, deciding they had enough money to go ahead. Big money interests now invested in the operation, as long as they could not buy it outright. This is the point where the careers of Ed Schieffelin and Bob Womack diverge.

By this time, all sorts of stores, offices and saloons had grown up near the diggings, and the motley collection had taken on the status of a city. Because of the slope of the land, streets were laid out at an angle from cardinal compass directions, numbered streets are intersected by Toughnut, Allen, Fremont and Safford. Allen became filled up first and remained the main street. The O. K. Corral, the Bird Cage Theater, Cosmopolitan Hotel, Campbell and Hatch's Pool Hall and many more places of dubious respectability mingled with stores along Allen Street.

The original prospectors, miners, assay men and other hard working gentry now gave way to a new crop of characters. This new crop was made up of men like Wyatt Earp, Doc Holliday, Bat Masterson, Luke Short and Turkey Creek Johnson. Johnson had come from Deadwood with a ready made reputation as a gunslinger, and his confidence in his own aim was such that he invited his opponents to meet him in front of the cemetery. Since he, himself, served as volunteer sexton, he figured to save himself some foot work.

The year 1880 alone saw 110 liquor licenses issued for honky tonks along Allen Street, until every other structure was a saloon. There were fourteen faro joints which never closed.

The biggest tide of population came sometime in the decade between 1880 and 1890, rising to about 15,000. Even with such a large proportion of the lawless, enough remained to support four churches, several dancing schools, along with a Masonic Hall, and quarters for the Knights of Pythias. Catering to culture was the Tombstone Club, this was a sort of library where many periodicals and books were rented, and where meetings were held to discuss plays, politics and the more genteel aspects of life in Tombstone. Somehow, these latter seem never to have been very prominent in the history of the place.

It seemed that there was an inexhaustible supply of silver in the mines, and the shafts went deeper and deeper. Then came catastrophe.

Abundant courses of water were encountered at these lower depths, and the mines filled. Huge pumps had to be installed. One, The Grand Central, stood thirty feet above its foundations and cost $300,000. It worked fine but the water went down slowly, in spite of an enormous outpouring at the mouth of the mine. Only when other mine owners began to celebrate did the horrible truth dawn. The Grand Central was draining all the mines in the district! Not only that, the others refused to share in the expense.

Pumping however, continued until 1885, when the old enemy, fire, struck and razed the pump house. A year later fire hit the Contention operations destroying the pumping works and forcing closure. Then, at long last—cooperation. A consolidated pumping system was set up and in 1901 sunk a main shaft to the depth of 1,080 feet, bringing out 8 million gallons of water a day. Tombstone got on its feet again and resumed the pleasures of the Bird Cage Theater, bawdy houses and saloons.

As the single male population had been increasing so had that of the prostitutes. A fair number of these were employed at the Bird Cage, where the girls acted as performers and danced with the customers "so as to promote friendly relations." Another group worked and lived in a house managed by a madame. Others, more independent or not up to the required standards, kept their own cribs, and sat at the doors to attract busi-

HEARSE MADE FREQUENT TRIPS to Boot Hill, sometimes several in one day as when Billy Clanton and McLowerys were buried there. Vehicle rented for those whose friends could afford it, where undertaker was employed and c a s k e t provided. More victims of bullets or mine accidents were merely laid in pine box and carried over. Even box was of skimpiest construction as lumber was a scarce and expensive commodity. Nearest timber was many miles away in high mountains. Any shipment of lumber had to be guarded as it came into town to prevent highjacking.

TOMBSTONE WAS ORIGIN-ALLY IN PIMA COUNTY, with seat at Tucson 73 miles across Whelstones. As town ex-panded in population, n e w county of Cochise was formed, and courthouse of adobe built on Fremont St. Increasing prestige demanded finer edifice, and this structure was put up at corner of Third and Toughnut Streets. It no longer serves, county seat having been transferred to Bis-bee.

ness. Still others walked the streets and went after customers avoiding a split of their earnings with a procurer.

Seldom did anyone hear of a surname for the girls. Nicknames prevailed, such as: Rowdy Kate, Dutch Annie, Blonde Marie, Irish May and Crazy Horse Lil. The land on which Dutch Annie built her brothels was owned by Wyatt Earp and leased to her.

The smaller respectable section, residences of families, etc., tried to edge as far as possible in the other corner of town, still not very far away, as too much expansion would go over the edge of the mesa.

This last flurry of boom and optimism was all too short, and signs of decay began to creep in when the inordinate cost of operating the pump-

ing system began to overtake income. The town was already on its last legs, when in 1914 the big Phelps Dodge Corporation bought equipment of the Tombstone Consolidated Mining Company at a receiver's sale for $50,000, sounding the death-knell of active mining for Tombstone.

The "town too tough to die" still lives, in a sense. It offers much to the visitor, a good many of the buildings so steeped in the rowdy history of the famous place still stand.

Ed Schieffelin lies now on the hill above town, near his first discovery. Over his grave is a stone marked "This is my Tombstone." His funeral was the largest ever held in town. The next largest was that of Dutch Annie, "Queen of the Red Light District," attracting a procession of 1,000 buggies, and most of the business men and city officials.

GLEESON, ARIZONA

The robin's-egg magic of turquoise lay hidden in the story of Gleeson but old Chief Cochise and the white man he trusted gave the town a gaudier color—blood red.

The Spanish had originally mined turquoise in the Dragoon Mountains as had a primitive race of Indians before them. The Spanish were a hard lot and subjected the aborigines to a state of slavery but were never able to extract from them the secret of where the real treasure of the blue-green gemstone lay. When the white man came and tried to win over the Indians with double-dealing tactics, Apache Chief Cochise, who had intended to be friendly if his tribe was let alone, rose up in all his savage wrath.

Up to 1860 Cochise had not actually molested any Americans but when he was taken into custody and accused of having conducted a raid on a ranch near the spot where the mining town of Gleeson was later built, he escaped his captors and made up for all the trouble he had not caused, spreading murder, rape and destruction among the ranchers.

For a long time he holed up in the Dragoons in an almost impregnable fortress. He held the U. S. Army at bay for ten years, yielding only through mediation with the one white man he trusted. This was Tom Jeffords who operated a stage on the old Butterfield line, long so vulnerable to Apache attack that drivers never traveled the route without an armed guard always on watch.

Jeffords had lost twenty-two of his men to the Apaches but nevertheless rode alone into the hideout of the old chief to see if he could arrange a peace. Cochise was so impressed with the man's bravery that he did pledge a personal pact with him and made him a blood brother. Jeffords was then able to negotiate a meeting between Cochise and General Howard. This resulted in a treaty, one of the terms being that Jeffords be made an Indian agent.

Shortly old Cochise died and was buried in the Dragoons. Only one white man knew just where and that was Tom Jeffords. He never revealed the secret although he lived forty years longer. The area was abundantly endowed with a type of live oak yielding an edible acorn, called "beyota"

OLD GLEESON GENERAL STORE was buy center of trade and word-of-mouth news when ranching and mining were important. The adobe building has coat of stucco for elegance. Louvre with fan for ventilation was added in days of electricity. Arcade with awnings of corrugated sheet metal was also latter day, luxury for loiterers on benches once lining wall. Live oaks gave shade and *beyotas* — edible acorns gathered by Apaches.

WELLS WERE NOT TOO DEPENDABLE in long dry summer of Dragoon Mountains. Town is filled with adobe ruins such as that of old saloon shown here, fallen to reveal view of Gleeson General Store.

OLD FASHIONED ICE BOX leans tipsily outside ruined house, well preserved in dry air. Shrub in background is mesquite, common in southwest desert areas. Belonging to legume family, nourishing seeds were ground, made into small cakes and baked for Indian's staple food. Plant grows into shrubby tree, is armed with vicious thorns, preventing cattle from grazing, is difficult to control.

by the Indians who gathered them in quantity everywhere but in Stronghold Canyon. It remained inviolate and would indicate this is the spiritland of the old chief.

With Indian troubles fading out the white man's thoughts again turned to the legends and tales of turquoise, gold, copper and silver to be found in the Dragoons. Some of all these treasures were located and the town that sprang up at the site of discovery was named Gleeson after one of the miners.

The town grew but never had a real boom. The area was already on a solid basis with cattle raising and moderate mining prosperity was taken in stride. The biggest boost to the economy came with the entry of Tiffany's of New York. This company proposed to mine turquoise on a big scale but the location of really valuable deposits remained elusive and after some desultory efforts, with only a small quantity of fine turquoise to show, Tiffany's left the scene. So did everyone else in time; even the cattle ranchers gave up as water grew more and more scarce. Only a family or two remain in the area.

ENTRANCE ARCH to old school. It had two large rooms, each holding about 30 pupils in four grades, served until 1945 when it was consolidated with Tombstone system. Now only student is small grandson of Senor Valdez who still lives in Gleeson, proudly claiming to own ruined jail. This had four cells, was wrecked by dynamite blast set off inside, blowing out all doors, windows and destroying roof. Other buildings were ruined by fire, vandals or time.

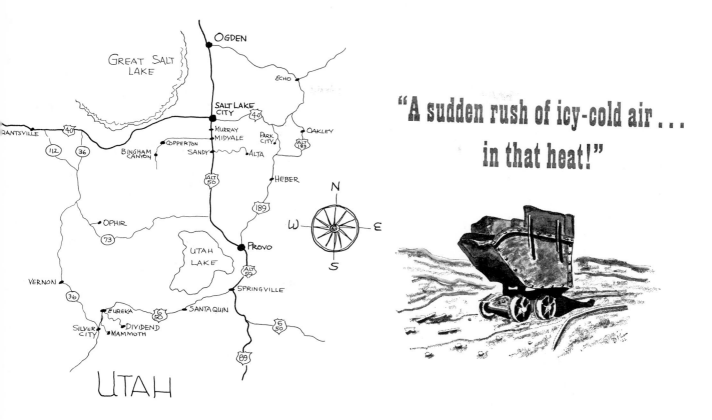

PARK CITY, UTAH

If the soldiers under Col. Patrick Connor could not find Indians to shoot at, they could always go prospecting. Dig into most of Utah mine history and you will find signs that many of the original discoveries were made by these far-cruising troopers in ragged, blue coats.

The phenomenal boom town of Park City is one that grew out of soldiers' finds. They ran across a bold outcropping of quartz, about two miles south of where the city would be built, and reported: "We tied a red bandana handkerchief to a bush where it could easily be seen to mark the place." The assay report for the chunk they brought to town stated there were 96 ounces of silver to the ton and goodly portions of gold and lead. A whole year passed before miners began working the claim and one conjectures—the soldiers were too busy looking for more to tell anybody what they had until 1870. Then a stampede for the peaceful meadows began.

Tents and brush shanties, always the first shelters in an embryo camp, soon lined the muddy "street" the length of the canyon. By the time the mud turned to dust miners built a boarding stable, meat market and most important, a saloon. The bar was a board laid over two kegs and on it a jug of rotgut and dipper—price of a dipper full, two bits. Later as a refinement a bottle of better

quality liquor with a glass or two and a shot of this was twice as much. A year later a mahogany bar was imported from Salt Lake City and with it the customary plate glass mirror and huge painting of a nude damsel reclining on a couch.

In ten years Park City had reached the status of a city in fact as well as name. 1884 saw rapid expansion in building, mining and shipping of ore. And here came the rowdy element. The editor of the *Park Record* complained: "There is too much promiscuous shooting going on in the streets at night." But in spite of shootings, brawls in the bistros and quarrels in the gambling houses, all was not evil in Park City. A Catholic church was built at the end of the first decade. A water system with a small reservoir and one pipe down the middle of the street was installed. Stages linked the town with others and there were signs a railroad, Rio Grande Western, was to run its rails this way.

When rumor of this became established fact, Park City "blew off its dusty lid," people ordinarily abstemious sharing in a great headache the next day. A more lasting worry was over the Chinese population suddenly swelled when the railroad decided not to use them in working crews.

Orientals never were popular with the miners largely because they could get along with so few

OLD HIGH SCHOOL dates back to days of first boom. Classes were still being held when prohibition came in, causing closure of 20 saloons and reducing revenue for city schools by $22,000 yearly. On that July day the miners tried to drink up the entire existing supply of liquor. Stocks were sold out 2 hours before deadline. Bartenders could not serve patrons fast enough so patrons served themselves. Some paid and some stole until at midnight the "grave digging bell" was tolled by the sexton himself warning all prohibition had come.

Frequently the table cloth caught fire, giving the volunteer fire department some practice. Another Chinese who had lived in the city a long time and had owned a business bringing him often in the public eye, rated an obituary in the *Park Record* which ended with some confusion as to his race. "He had been ailing for a long time as though simply to save funeral expenses. He was buried by his fellow 'chinks' . . . with his hat on so he would not catch cold on his way to his Happy Hunting Grounds."

All this time the mining activities had burgeoned to the point where the populace became smug over their future, claiming "Park City is about to become the first city in Utah, will soon outstrip Salt Lake City itself." Then came bad times from an unexpected source.

The first rich workings had been shallow, easily worked and caused the big boom. As the good ores went deeper and became more refractory, miners had difficulty keeping up with the changing conditions. Then as workings reached greater depths

comforts and work for so little money. Some went into businesses of their own, laundries and opium dens the most popular. One laundryman, desiring privacy for his afternoon pipe of poppy juice, always crawled under the table with a lighted candle.

POLICE AND FIRE DEPARTMENT buildings were recently repaired and painted after long period of neglect. Modern alarm was installed on hose tower, replacing old bell. Fires plagued Park City, worst one in 1898. Blaze started in hotel dining room, took most of town, cost $1 million. Arson was suspected, *Park Record* reported: "Should anyone be caught setting fire to a building, his life would not be worth a straw. Murder may be committed, the law allowed to take its course, but the line is drawn on the fire bug and God help the man. . . . A long rope and a short shrift will be his portion as a fate."

OLD SCHOOL stands on higher level street, is slowly being dismantled. Signs warn of falling bricks. Period of reform lasted several years, making deep inroads in revenue for school upkeep; gambling and wide open saloons returned in 1909, easing maintenance of public buildings. Second reform then took over, every den of vice except saloons being closed. Temperance worker told *Record* he "watched the leading saloon and counted the men going in and out, from 7:30 p.m. to 8:30 p.m. The result was 153 in and 164 out."

they got to the water table. One by one the mines became flooded and had to be abandoned. The town was about to die when the big mine owners saw the light; instead of battling each other over conflicting claims, thus supporting an army of lawyers, they joined forces. With combined capital, drainage tunnels were dug, the water removed and Park City got back to work.

At the turn of the century methods of getting at ores had lost most of the grief and sadness of earlier days but the *Park Record* kept the people informed. In 1905 it said: "Twelve years ago two old time prospectors, while exploring a small drift at the bottom of a shaft, stumbled on the body of a man . . . the heavy shoes . . . enclosed gruesomely the shiny bones of the feet . . . a sheet of paper was found upon which was written in a faltering and uncertain hand a short but pitiful story. 'Dear God, I am dying. I have found wealth at the cost of my life. The samples in the bucket are from a ledge on—my hand trembles, my eyes grow dim—I—I am.' Here the record becomes a senseless jumble."

The *Park Record* was always the lead news-

paper. Others had succeeded for a time, the *Call* coming out in 1887 and dying in eighteen months. *The Miner* ran for two years, the *Utah Patriot Miner* holding on for a like period and the *Park Miner* printed its little sheet from 1902 to 1903. Editorials in all the papers were often fiery, sometimes vituperative attacks on people freely identified by name. A customary practice was to air the personal life of some prominent individual or candidate for public office. Libel laws if any were vague but every now and then an infuriated citizen would personally assault an editor in a fusillade of gunfire on the street or in the office of the paper. No staff man seems to have been lost to the *Park Record* however.

One of the services of this stalwart was a hybrid column, a cross between "personals" and "help wanted." During the hard times of 1897, appeared this pathetic plea: "A competent sawmill man wishes a situation. Can run a sawmill and keep it in repair from engine to slab pile. P. S. If I cannot get a situation in a mill, would be perfectly willing to accept a situation with some widow (no matter how grassy) until the roses bloom again."

ALTA, UTAH

In all innocence and guile, one legend says, the lady picked up a piece of ore and asked: "Is this what you are looking for?" The men stood open-mouthed. It was just exactly what they were looking for—a chunk of silver-bearing quartz. And it set off the wildest rush of prospectors Utah had ever seen.

"They"—the gopher-nosed, metal-minded soldiers of Col. Patrick E. Connor's regiment—had been officially mapping the canyon but probing the cliff sides for rich rock was more to their fancy. The canyon and the area around it was a favorite Indian hunting ground until the natives were forced out by white trappers in the 1830s, but they seldom climbed the sides of the defiles as high as this spot where the wife of the party's surgeon found the piece of argentiferous galena in 1864.

This was Little Cottonwood Canyon which drops from its elevation of 8,583 feet to Alta to debouch upon the plain a few miles from Salt Lake City. It cuts a spectacular gorge deep in the Wasatch Mountains, with sides so steep that avalanches are

BEAUTIFUL SLOPES OF LITTLE COTTONWOOD CANYON bear deep scars of mining operations in heyday of Alta. Remains of town are seen at lower right, where lift towers of modern ski resort stand. Skiers are carried directly over what is left of once booming town of 5,000 people. Railroad had just reached camp as death throes took over, failed to share in prosperity, also died. Grade made excellent bed for spectacular road which now carries throngs of skiers to popular Alta Resort.

COVERED TRAM extends from mouth of silver mine to chute. Ore dropped down chute to bunker, collecting until load was ready for wagons and long dangerous haul down precipitous grade to plain below. There smelters awaited where earlier ore had to be shipped overseas for treatment. Alpine area offers much beauty, pointed firs and spruces, spread far apart make parklike scene, spaces between trees filled by wild flowers in short summer season.

frequent, especially early in spring. It is formed of granite of such beauty that the stone for Mormon Temple was quarried from near its mouth.

The first prospectors were almost poverty-stricken, few with any large stakes and the whole group of them was nearly starved out before they could get their claims going on a producing basis. For example, J. P. Woodman, who located what would be the fabulous Emma, which later was sold for $5,000,000, was so hard pressed for capital at the start that he offered a one-quarter interest in the holding for $3,000, and got no takers.

For lack of milling equipment, Woodman and his hungry crew "rawhided" the best ore, wrapping it in green cow hides. Hauling it down the canyon on ox-drawn wagons and "stone boats," thence to Ogden. From there it was shipped to San Francisco, loaded on sailing vessels which carried it around the Horn to Swansea, Wales, where it was milled and smelted. Even after the cost of all this transportation was deducted, there was still $180 a ton left over for Woodman and his men.

Armed with these statistics, he went to Walker Brothers, Salt Lake City grocery firm and sold them one-sixth interest for $25,000, and a Mr. Hussey, a fourth interest for the same amount. What Walker Brothers thought of this deal is not recorded.

After further indication of potential wealth of the Emma, the several partners got together and

sold the mine to a firm of investors called Parks and Baxter. The next step in this game of high finance, on receipt of option, was Parks going to Washington, D. C. interesting President Grant and through him gaining the attention of the Prime Minister of England, Mr. Schenk. This worthy bought in for $50,000, thus becoming a director of the combine. Eastern interests eagerly put in $375,000 for a half interest and then everybody got together and formed The Emma Mining Company of New York.

Now the whole operation moved overseas and in England, details of such a prodigous pouring out of silver from the Emma inspired the forming of the Emma Silver Mining Company, Ltd. of London. They purchased the entire interest for the sum of $5,000,000.

All this time the Emma had been faithfully producing its immense quantities of silver. But, almost at the same instant the huge deal was consummated, its output was suddenly cut off. The vein had run up against a solid wall of granite, broken off by faulting.

The outcry of fraud was loud and English investors protested so volubly that a board of investigation had to be set up in order to avoid an international incident.

The board found that there had been no collusion, that no one could have foreseen the pinching out of the lode. The many investors were left

SNOWS **R E A C H IMMENSE DEPTHS** in canyon high in Wasatch Mountains as shown by tower door for crawling into cabin when regular entrance was blocked. In case one didn't know, door carries lettering, "Winter Enterence."

to unhappily lick their wounds. For a long time after that, American mining stock found very poor sale in England.

Back in Alta, however, less touted mines like the Wasatch, Alta Consolidated, North Star, Prince of Wales and others had been producing steadily, if less gaudy amounts. Their best ore was now processed in new smelters a few miles out on the plain. The '80s produced some $13,000,000 worth of silver.

During all this time a boom had been going on in Alta. By 1872 the town had gathered a population of 5,000. There were 26 saloons, the most popular of which were the Bucket of Blood and the Gold Miner's Daughter. A gallon of whiskey cost $9, but it was one of the necessities of life. The usual "frail sisters" drifted in and out solicit-

ing their trade. Organized houses of prostitution also flourished, presided over by Alta Nell, Katie Hayes and others. These Madams held high places in a community predominately populated by young males, and one of the larger mines was named for Katie.

Snowfall reached extreme depths in this mountain camp, and in order to promptly dispose of casualties in the brothels and saloons where brawls and shootings were common, a tunnel was kept open to the cemetery.

In the '70s, production fell off to a mere $1,703,-068, and the following year Alta was hard put to make a million. Things were already at a low ebb when demonetization of silver hit in '93 and nearly finished the town. Continuing avalanches which killed many and destroyed much property did.

MAMMOTH, UTAH

Not every day could the pioneers say: "With a bunch of cows the McIntyres made two million." The fortune was not in milk but a mine—the Mammoth. At its peak of production it poured out $1,000 worth of ore to the ton.

But this was some time in happening. Originally staked in 1871, it remained unworked for two years due to the inhospitable combination of Indians, dry weather and barren country. When the owners, Charles Crismon and partners, did make some developments, they had only mediocre success. Discouraged but alert, Crismon saw an opportunity to unload his share on the gullible McIntyre brothers.

Sam and William McIntyre were driving a herd of Texas Longhorn cattle to market at Salt Lake City and were searching for good range land on which to fatten the animals a little before the last leg of the drive. But falling in with Crismon, the brothers were much impressed with the mine owner's glowing description of the wealth that awaited some lucky man who would buy the Mammoth, invest some money in it and sink the main shaft to the point where it would meet with a fabulous lode of silver.

Sam and William decided to trade their cattle for the biggest share of the mine. Crismon continued to market with his animals and the brothers did exactly as they were supposed to do. They did spend some money developing the property, sank the shaft deeper and just as their truthful friend had predicted, met up with the fabulous vein.

Some shady developments with surprising results took place in the district with the legitimate success of the Mammoth. A Mr. Pease, becoming discouraged with his Wyoming mine devised a method of "salting" it for the benefit of a couple of innocent gentlemen who wished "to buy a good mine." Before showing these men the property Pease purchased two carloads of rich ore from the Eureka Hill and dumped the valuable raw material down the shaft. The sale was then readily consummated, Pease to receive $20,000 cash and the remaining balance of $2,000 in a week's time. The new owners saved the final payment, of course— Pease was no longer around to collect. On the strength of the kind of ore they had taken out of the shaft, the operators first constructed a mill. When the rich ore in the hole had been put through it, there was no more to process. As further exploratory probing went on, the owners were forced

to take in custom milling to keep from going broke; then suddenly began to break into paying veins, one of which yielded more than $1,000,000.

Another case of salting was performed in reverse. A superintendent placed a lot of worthless ore around the mouth of the mine and informed the owners that the whole thing was hopeless. He would, however, take a lease on it at a very reasonable price and work on it in his spare time. This he did, soon getting down to the lode he knew was there all along.

The turn of the century saw a period of wild living, robberies, holdups and killings. Two miners, William Dryburn and Barney Dunne were spending a quiet Sunday in 1902 getting drunk in their tent. An argument developed as to who was the better shot. Dryburn dared the other to see if he, Dunne could shoot Dryburn's hat off. Dunne proved to be an even worse marksman than his partner had thought, the rifle bullet found its mark in the middle of Dryburn's forehead.

The Mammoth Mine had been performing well. The McIntyres had built twenty-two furnace smelters and Sam had constructed a mansion, a fine brick home in the town of 1,000 that had grown up around his mine.

When the richest ores were exhausted and the poorer ones failed to pay the milling and smelting costs, the mills closed down and people began to move away. Even the Mammoth operations ceased and Sam left his brick house to wandering cowboys and sheepherders. The big schoolhouse was boarded up for many years and finally torn down, the swings in the playgrounds remaining at one side of the rubble and the basketball hoop on the other.

ORE CARS ONCE KEPT BUSY at Mammoth Mine now stand rusting on tracks narrower than regular ore car gauge. Cars, however, are standard one-ton size, so that amount of ore from mine could be calculated.

SILVER CITY, UTAH

Silver City was the first real mining camp established in the famous district known as Tintic, after the Indian chief who made so much trouble for the early settlers who were fouling up the Ute's streams and killing their game. For years after it was founded in 1870 it dropped out of importance because more spectacular strikes in Little Cottonwood Canyon and Park City were getting all the attention.

The hopeful but brief life of Silver City began when, in 1869, cowboy George Rust found remains of age-old mines worked by primitive Indians. Without explosive of any kind these early miners managed to penetrate the rocks and dig crude tunnels for long distances, carrying out the ore in skin bags. Evidence seemed to point to a system of fires built against the head of the workings until the rock was hot, then cold water thrown against it to make it crack. One such old mine discovered in the '20s had several large boulders piled against the entrance. When these were rolled away, two human skeletons were exposed.

The Utes, under Chief Tintic, seemed to know nothing about precious metals and care less. But George Rust did. He managed to dodge enough Indian bullets to make a silver discovery. During the summer of the next year a group of five men found promising pieces of float. With assay offices few and far between, it was December before they had a report and this was exciting enough to send them into a blinding blizzard to stake the claim. It was named the Sun Beam and was the forerunner of a dozen or more rich locations in the district.

Laid out at the mouth of Dragon Canyon, the young camp of Silver City dragged its feet for a year or two because of lack of capital. Here were no easy panning and placering methods to return wealth for little outlay of money, but much labor in hard rock mining, blasting out the material and lifting it to the tops of shafts. I. E. Diehl described Silver City and its slow start in his Tintic manuscript, "A billiard saloon, blacksmith shop, grog hole, some tents, several drunks, a free fight, water some miles off, a hole down 90 feet hunting a spring without success, and any number of rich or imaginary rich lodes in the neighborhood. The owners are all poor and poor men work for them. By next spring the poor will be poorer."

Economic conditions slowly improved to the point where about 800 people were making a modest living. About the time their hard-won shafts began penetrating real blossom rock, disaster struck; water began filling the workings, stopping operations almost entirely. William Hatfield managed to get enough water out of the Swansea to salvage ore to the tune of $700,000 and when some of those who had abandoned the town heard about this they returned to see if they could equal the feat in their own claims. But no—pumping cost more than value received and again they quit. That was final and when Hatfield also quit the town was finished. Today not one of the original buildings stands on the site, though several newer ones attest to recent efforts to again reopen the flooded mines.

ONLY RELIC REMAINING FROM EARLY DAYS OF SILVER CITY Tottering head frame and loading bunker. Extensive tailings and refuse dumps attest to large amount of ore removed during active days. Road, now clogged by tailings, used to run under bunker, wagon loads to be conveyed to smelter. Typical desert vegetation covers hill sides. Shrubby trees in background are Utah juniper.

EUREKA, UTAH

Water and life had spiritual significance. The earth was not to be spoiled by digging into it. The spirits would not like that and much harm could come to a man if he angered them.

At least that was the Indian point of view and Tintic was a good Indian, a Ute chief. The valley was well watered by many streams, grass grew thick and tall. Deer and antelope were plentiful and occasionally the braves trapped a buffalo herd. What Tintic and the rest of his village people did not like was the white men poking around in the rocks as if they meant to find something and stay there. He led raiding parties on the white settlers' tents, fired on them and drove them away —but they always came back with twice as many men.

Stage drivers and lone Pony Express riders claimed the valley was the wildest and most dan-

gerous on the whole route. Cattle men would have stayed away entirely but for all that fine grass and water. It was good grazing in spite of the cattle thefts by Tintic's warriors. And the white settlement grew so large Tintic finally gave up, and went to Manti where he died in 1859.

The little streams in the valley, clear and lovely, were adequate for watering the natural vegetation but when big mining operations got under way, they were woefully deficient. Certainly there was none left for domestic use and for a long time water was hauled into Eureka and sold for ten cents a gallon. Then a wooden pipeline was built from Jenny Lind Spring. This emptied into a vat in the center of town, from which the water was carried home in pails by householders. This primitive system had to suffice until '93 when a line was installed from Cherry Creek which allowed piping to many individual homes. When water was first turned into the new system there was a celebration lasting all night, and the liquid consumed was not water!

Eureka had its "characters." One of these was one Matteo Messo, born in Sonora, Mexico. He came to Utah with Johnston's army, winding up in the mining camp of Ophir. After a few years of hard work there he "struck it rich" and retired to Eureka. With more money than he could spend he nevertheless couldn't break old habits of economy and continued to "roll his own." As each bag of Bull Durham was emptied it was carefully hung on one of the rafters of his little cabin, "to keep the evil spirits away." But he gave away thousands of dollars to derelicts and beggars, finally dying in the little cabin, broke. The whole ceiling was filled with the little empty tobacco bags.

There was "Buffalo Davis," who made a good stake, soon losing it via the bottle. When every cent was gone he sold his body to a medical so-

HEAD FRAME above one of more recently operated mines in Eureka. At top are sheaves on which ropes and cables lowered or lifted men and ore buckets. Latter caught on tripper above chute, causing bucket to dump contents into waiting wagon. Underground, mile-long drifts required more than manpower to haul one-ton ore cars. Mules were often used. Underfed to reduce weight and legs strapped tightly to sides, animal was lowered in vertical position to workings. Once down it spent remainder of life in darkness.

ciety, and when those funds were also gone he was sent to an asylum in Provo and shortly died.

John Q. Packard couldn't bring himself to spend the necessary quarter to ride the twenty miles from Santaquin to Eureka so he walked, even when the weather was bad. Yet, when he died he left provisions for a library in Salt Lake, the lot to cost $20,000 and the building $100,000. In addition, he left an estate of $20,000,000.

Best remembered for eccentricities, however, is Mrs. Anna Marks. She was a Russian Jewess and came to Eureka in the '80s. Settling herself in the big boarding house on the main street, she attracted no particular attention. Then one night, when a sufficiently large crowd had gathered, she came screaming out, sobbing that the Chinese owner of the boarding house had raped her. Though she had no friends in the town, sentiment against Orientals was so strong that she had no difficulty in getting the embarrassed Cantonese arrested on her testimony. He escaped and fled the town. As soon as he was gone, the crafty lady took over the boarding house operation and did very well with it. Her next door neighbor was John Cronin who made the mistake of stepping on her side of the property line. Her violent abuse made him decide to build a board fence between them. As soon as he had a few post holes dug Mrs. Marks in a fury, grabbed a shovel and filled them in. As he proceeded she got into one of the holes and Cronin calmly dumped dirt on top of her. The affair developed by these means into a knock down, drag out fight, ending when Cronin threw her to the ground and sat on her. The irate woman rushed to court again, but by this time her reputation had preceded her and police refused even to arrest Cronin.

Another unwitting trespasser was Harvey Tompkins, who owned the hotel on the other side. He also attempted to build a "spite fence." Mrs. Marks' recourse this time was to get a gun and start shooting. Fortunately for Tompkins, he was not a smoker; the lady's first well-aimed shot found its mark in a large plug of tobacco in his pants pocket, causing him to temporarily abandon the fence building project. The Rio Grande Railroad was the next victim. The line attempted to build a spur across the corner of her property and was forced to make a heavy settlement on her for the privilege. Although contending the land wasn't legally hers, the company couldn't pursuade its workmen to face the indomitable woman and her gun. Eureka breathed easier when in 1912 Mrs. Marks died, worth $70,000.

BINGHAM CANYON, UTAH

Brigham Young was not about to have his flock foresake farming for mining. So, when Sanford and Thomas Bingham found gold and other metals in the canyon they had been sent to cultivate, and when news of their dereliction seeped back to headquarters, a proper reprimand was soon dispatched to the boys. "Instead of hunting gold," the message read, "let every man go to work at raising wheat, oats, barley, corn and vegetables in abundance that there may be plenty in the land." The brothers, being good Mormons, covered up their prospect holes, though not without regrets.

This episode transpired in 1848 and about the only visible traces of it are the bare slopes on both sides of the canyon, denuded by busy axes and mills operated by the Binghams.

The next stage in the canyon's history came in 1863, the year Col. Patrick Connor was taking such an intense interest in Utah's mineral wealth. His legitimate business was flushing Indians out of hiding places in the canyons of the Wasatch and neighboring ranges but he could not resist looking for "float" too. The colonel's side line had reached farmers of Bingham Canyon, and one of them sent him a piece of ore thrown out of the early prospect diggings of the Bingham brothers and their friends. This chunk of galena turned out to be rich in silver and gold. That was the smoke signal. The rush was on. In a wave of goodwill, the colonel issued a letter on War Department stationery, informing the general public of the find and personally guaranteeing safety to all who wished to stake out claims in this canyon or any other in the area.

Bingham Canyon history from this point is the reverse of what almost every other mining camp experienced. The hard-rock work was begun first, because of the nature of that first sample, and there was enough encouragement from the results to get a boom town on its feet, though none too steadily. Ores proved refractory in the face of scanty and expensive milling equipment. Heavy losses took place, most of the precious metals "going down the drain." The miners decided to ship the ore somewhere else, like Swansea, Wales, for refining, and some of it actually did go that far. But to make that sort of shipping pay, the raw stuff had to be as rich as it was in Alta, in the Wasatch mountains, and this it was not. So the camp began to die almost as soon as it was born. Then came the discovery that there was a bonanza

in the gravels of the canyon, with little expense in the gathering of this wealth. Placering was then started up and down the canyon's length and the town was saved.

Now things began to happen in a big way. One of the placers, the Clay bar, turned out some $100,-000 by 1868, and when the owners stopped at water level they turned their attention to the tailings dumps abandoned in early operations. Each of the men stacked up about ten dollars a day, and every so often a nugget came to light. One was the largest ever found in Utah, worth $128. Altogether, some $2,500,000 in gold was placered out of the gulches by 1870, when the Bingham and Camp Floyd Railroad reached town.

This event brought about some drastic changes, since it occurred about the same time the gravels began to show signs of depletion. Cheaper trans-

LITTLE JAIL AT REAR OF POLICE STATION was popular, full up on weekends, jammed at Christmas. Prisoners were not always drunks. One Rafael Lopez arrived in Bingham as a strikebreaker in 1912, nearly killed a Greek in savage fight over girls. After release from jail, he was again in girl trouble. He shot a rival, Juan Valdez, and took to the hills, evading posse after killing three pursuers, backtracked to town, took refuge in mine. During efforts to smoke him out another officer was killed. After five days, smoke cleared away but fugitive had vanished.

portation changed the picture for hard-rock men and it wasn't long before many tons of good ore were headed for the mills, which by this time had been established on the plain. Again the sagging economy of Bingham experienced an upsurge, the population going from 276 to more than 1,000. Substantial frame buildings replaced flimsy shanties. As earning power increased, easier ways were found to help the miners spend their money. "Share-the-wealth programs" burgeoned in more honky tonks and gambling houses, more hook joints and cribs, than even Brigham Young had feared would materialize when he first heard of metal in the hills. The narrow canyon and one narrow street echoed day and night with sounds of revelry. Shifts in the mines were on a continuous basis and there were always plenty of off-duty men looking for a change of pace. By 1900 there were 30 saloons, and among some twenty brands of whiskey, the top two were "Old Crow" and "16 to 1." The first moving pictures were shown in these dives, Mary Pickford in "Little Lord Fauntleroy" having a long run.

The easing of transportation problems, which made it economically feasible to ship ore out for refining, also made it possible to ship in the materials and parts for mills and smelters. As soon as some of these were completed, ore ceased to flow out of town, being replaced by the finished product. Erection of the Winnamuck Smelter in '72 and '73 by the Nevada-experienced firm of Bristol and Bateman was a big step forward in lode mining, as was A. H. Bemis' concentration plant treatment of lead ore. Biggest strikes were at the Yosemite No. 1, Brooklyn, No-You-Don't, Highland Boy, and Boston Consolidated.

The depression of 1893 almost closed the camp with bottom prices for silver, lead and gold. Bingham miners had always been conscious of some copper in almost all ores taken out of the canyon but it was usually scorned—heavy percentage of copper sulphide caused an upset in orderly extraction of gold. Now, with the old standbys fallen on evil days, with amounts of copper increasing, even up to 18 per cent, that metal could be ignored no longer. Small shipments of copper had been made as early as 1896, but now at the turn of the century, it began to assume a major role.

At this time the Highland Boy merged with the Utah Consolidated. After further deals involving $12,000,000, the now huge copper mines were controlled by one John D. Rockefeller. The next big change was in 1907, when deep shafts were abandoned, since copper was everywhere, and only "scooping" was necessary. (Open pit mining is the practice to this day). A merger with other companies created a new group with $100,000,000 behind it.

The town in the narrow canyon suffered disaster, natural and man-caused. Avalanches of snow and mud slid down the slopes left bare by Brigham Young's men, inundating whole sections of town, and killing many. Fires raged unchecked among tinder dry frame structures and floods rushed down the gulch, washing entire buildings out onto the plain. The town hordes survived all these but now a deliberate annihilation is its certain fate. The old narrow street has not been able to properly carry traffic for several years, so street, houses and buildings all must give way to a broad highway, to carry the flood tide of modern miners.

OLD CITY HALL—POLICE STATION building s e r v e d Bingham Canyon many years, stood at edge of small parking lot at head of Canyon road. Above are mile after mile of dumps, surmounted by tracks bearing dump cars, endlessly carrying out waste, extending dumps to far hillsides, burying cacti and juniper trees. Operation goes on with complete indifference to day or night.

OPHIR, UTAH

Before Ophir were the Indians. They ranged the narrow canyon and made bullets from the silver they mined. In 1865 Col. Patrick E. Connor's far-ranging troops heard about the fancy slugs and routed the redmen at the source of them. The lode was in East Canyon, a slit in the mountains shadowed early and late by tiered, castellated cliffs. The soldiers named the place St. Louis.

By 1870 it became necessary to form a new mining district and plat a town. Both were romantically christened Ophir for the fabulous mines of King Solomon and such individual mine names as Wild Delirium and Miner's Delight indicated high spirits. On August 23, 1870, horn silver was found on Silverado Hill and in rapid order the Silveropolis, Chloride Point and Shamrock lodes were staked out. With the Ophir and Pocatello already producing in a big way, the town zoomed into something resembling a frenzy.

Almost overnight the narrow, dusty canyon trail was lined with tents, saloons, brothels and then stores, a small hotel which was a hybrid of whipsawed lumber and canvas, and two slapped-together restaurants. The first silver ore from the Silveropolis assayed $24,000 to the ton in ten car lots and a dozen new claims were located on Lion and Tiger Hills.

Most often boom camp optimism received a set back when the time came to build a mill and the ore was found to be refractory. Ophir's ores however went through the first mill, built by Walker Brothers of Salt Lake City, with the greatest of ease. The operators saved about eighty percent of the metal where in some early mills all but about twenty-five percent was lost. The first mill was called the Pioneer and its success inspired the erection of several others, among them the Brevoort and Enterprise. Smelters were the next logical step and the Ophir and Faucet were put up.

Tents were replaced by more substantial structures and the easy-going success of Ophir's affairs inspired some fancy stone and brick houses. And years later, when the silver deposits were exhausted and Ophir died, the buildings stood out like mausoleums pointing up the town's short life.

From time to time new life was breathed into the corpse and Ophir sat up again. Copper and zinc in the diggings proved almost equal to silver in value. Some mines here were almost as permanent as the one operated for twenty-five years by Senator W. A. Clark of Montana and Marcus Daly's Zella. In the '30s the International Smelting and Refining Co. built a 600-ton flotation mill at the mouth of the canyon to treat the 400,000 tons of tailings from the old Ophir Mining Co.

POST OFFICE FOR PERMANENT CITY which wasn't. One of solid structures erected when townspeople thought Ophir would be stable. Large sums of money and bullion were handled in one section used as bank, necessitating iron shutters and doors as protection from Indians, bandits. During later, transient boom building served as tavern, bore simple sign reading "Beer."

"Stunted growths . . . bleached white . . . like skeletons!"

TUMCO, CALIFORNIA

Stark desert is the setting for the battered ruins of Tumco. Summers are witheringly hot for humans in the sandy wastes at the edge of the Cargo Muchacho Mountains. The small canyon, holding what is left of the camp, is twenty-five miles from Yuma, Arizona, where the thermometer often reaches 110 degrees or more. Winters offer luxurious temperatures of 60 to 80 with so much bright sunshine a Yuma resort offered "Free meals and lodging any day the sun doesn't shine."

Indians in prehistoric times carved petroglyphs on the canyon rocks near the twin cones of the Cargo Muchachos. The summit of these peaks is a bare 2,000 feet in elevation but they give the illusion of greater height because of the extremely low flat country, much of which in the nearby Imperial Valley is actually below sea level. Early Indians did considerable crude mining, as well as using the blackish "desert varnish" on the rocks. Their comings and goings to the mine sites and "picture galleries" were so constant their bare feet made conspicuous trails on the rocky ground, paths easily traced by the lighter color where the ancient patina has worn off. Along these primitive tracks are sometimes found potsherds and other artifacts.

From 1865 to 1870 Mexicans found gold in the gravels of Jackson Gulch but kept the discovery to themselves, working the area in a quiet and self-contained way. Production was low and not enough gold was brought into Yuma to cause a stir. A spark of excitement came in the early

'80s—news of a find made by a track walker named Hedges. He was apparently more interested in prospecting than sprung rails as his discovery was made in a canyon some distance from the railroad, a few gulches away from the Mexican claims—mica schist heavily laced with gold. Hedges promptly set a stake, quit his job with a small crew, set up mining operations on an enterprising scale.

Several methods of refining the gold were employed, first with crushing mills ranging up from one or two stamps to the hundred stamp mill considered to be one of the largest in the west, if not the world. Final recovery was generally accomplished in cyanide vats. The finished gold bars were hauled to the railroad at Ogilby, shipped to San Francisco mint.

The town growing up at the scene of the diggings was named after its founder and soon had over three thousand people. Water was piped in from Pilot Knob on the Colorado River. Hedges had all the trappings of the boom town except for the usual hotel, the men living in cabins of wood or stone, the natural building material as nothing was more abundant than rocks in this region so barren of soil, water and vegetation. Hedges had its Chinaman—Charley Sam who ran a grocery store.

During the town's period as Hedges it was free of the early day violence but it was responsible for one tragedy it would like to have forgotten. A handsome Mexican boy named Pedro

78

HOUSE IS QUAINT EXAMPLE of building with material at hand. Lumber for roof, lintels, etc., was imported, walls constructed of stones picked up within few feet, mud from desert floor holding them together, whole plastered with lime mortar.

worked at the twenty stamp mill at the entrance of a small side canyon. The adjacent cyanide plant had turned out three glistening gold bars in the morning but after lunch the men discovered there were only two in evidence. Pedro, being a "Mex" and handy, was promptly accused of the theft, but he vigorously denied any guilt. The men, determined to force an admission, tied his thumbs together and fastened them to the end of a rope thrown over a beam of the stamp mill. The rope was drawn taught. Still the boy protested his innocence. The men pulled some more until he was suspended, screaming with pain. Still no confession was forthcoming and he was lowered, only to have the rope made into a noose and placed around his neck. He was then forced to stand on a beam, the slack in the rope again taken up. Once again he was questioned, and promised that if he would tell where the bar was hidden he would be freed. The boy repeated

WRECK OF HUGE STAMP MILL comprising one hundred stamps, said to be one of the largest in the West. (Another of one hundred stamps stood at Melones in the Mother Lode country until it burned in 1942.) Mill was designed and built by '49ers who profited by mistakes in hard rock mines in Mother Lode where first crushers had square wooden stems and square iron shoes with no way of rotating them, a serious flaw as ore had to be broken by hand and shoveled into mill.

OGILBY, few miles from Tumco, was railroad shipping point for finished gold bars to San Francisco mint. In its heyday Ogilby was wild place, rowdiness not tolerated at Tumco mines. Men came here to spend money in honky tonks. With end of mining activity and close of Tumco, Ogilby languished and died. Buildings were hauled away or wrecked. When this photo was made in '61, only small shack remained near tiny cemetery. In '62 even this was gone and grave enclosures had been used for firewood.

he knew nothing about it. In a rage, several of the men gave the boy a shove and after a few convulsive jerks he was dead. Years later, when the mill was dismantled, a bar of gold was found in the foundations.

When Hedges was satisfied with his profits and tired of mining, he sold the whole operation to the Borden of condensed milk fame. Borden carried on under a corporation called The United Mining Company. He took the initials of the name and made Tumco of them, and so renamed the town. Ore became more and more free milling so that his profits increased as long as expenses were low. Then came the turn in events that caused so many camps to die, increasing costs while the price of gold remained fixed.

Borden closed down in 1909, and sold everything in the place. Machinery was hauled to Ogilby and shipped out, what little good lumber existed there was salvaged, and another ghost town came into being. Tumco today is a forlorn, completely deserted ruin. Particularly pathetic is the cemetery, well populated for a small town. Because of the acute water shortage, many mining operations were carried out dry when the drills and crushers should have been bathed in water. The dust penetrated lungs, resulting in what was called "miner's consumption" and was in time fatal. Excavations for graves were of the shallowest in this rocky terrain—a few inches had to suffice. Then rocks were piled up to form a cover about two feet high. These graves laid out appear in rows on a flat without a blade of grass or vegetation other than a few ocotillos and a little sparse grease-wood. Only one grave now has a splinter of wood which was once a cross. There is no identification on any of them, and a more lonely, barren and desolate resting place cannot be imagined.

BLEAK AND DESOLATE are crumbling ruins of adobe store building. Material for unfired bricks was hauled up from desert floor, walls covered with lime mortar stucco. Cargo Muchacho (Errand Boy) Range rises abruptly at rear of building, lacking any earth or tree covering.

THE MOTHER LODE

No part of our country has a richer tradition or more fabulous history than a narrow stretch of Sierra Piedmont extending along the western slope from Mariposa to the Yuba River. That rainy day of January, 1848, when James Marshall burst in on John A. Sutter at Sutter's Fort stuttering almost incoherently a tale of his finding gold in the mill-race of Sutter's sawmill at Coloma, meant the end of "the happiest period any country ever knew."

Certainly it spelled the end of Sutter's vast domain, his agricultural empire, depleted of help when almost every man left for the gold fields. This particular incident was perhaps not vital to California as a whole but it signalled the end of a period, of the state's "Golden Age of Innocence." It meant the beginning of another kind of golden age, one which produced some $750 million in actual gold, part of it in chunks weighing as much as 195 pounds.

At first all the yellow metal was found loose in the stream beds, placer gold in the form of dust and small nuggets. When this easily garnered supply dwindled, the Argonauts had to start scratching and in many cases found the veins from which the loose stuff was weathering away. The Mexicans who were working the southern end of the strip called this vein, "La Veta Madre," and so the origin of the term, "Mother Lode," which came to apply more directly to that part of the gold bearing band between Mariposa and El Dorado. There is no geographical division between The Mother Lode, or Southern Mines, and the Northern Mines but an arbitrary line is usually drawn in the neighborhood of El Dorado or Placerville.

The author's treatment of this southern section by no means includes every Gold Rush town but is a generous and typical sampling both of well known ones and others off Highway 49, the main connecting link. The Northern Mines will be similarly covered in another volume and will include Coloma, Georgetown, Colfax, Dutch Flat and others.

MARIPOSA, CALIFORNIA

The miners wanted to work and the Indians wanted revenge and loot. The latter raided the camps in trails of blood and the miners couldn't leave their families long enough to make pay dirt. So the story Charles Smithers heard until he died at 85 was part of the Mariposa pattern.

He was a baby when his father made a trip on horseback from Mariposa to one of the nearby mining camps. 25-year-old father Smithers completed his errand safely but on the way home his horse skittered and looking back, he saw several Indians following him. Spurring his horse he galloped straight into an ambush and as he tried to ride free, an arrow pierced his thigh, pinning his leg to the saddle. Nauseated by pain and loss of blood, he made it back to Mariposa where he fell from his horse, dragging the arrow through his leg.

Shortly after this bands of natives stationed themselves at strategic points around the town and other camps, levying tribute from all white travelers. James D. Savage, who owned three trading posts, one on the banks of the creek at Mariposa, had spearheaded a movement to rid the area of Indians and they retaliated by looting and burning his stores. Now thoroughly aroused, a large group of American miners and others organized a war party and took out after them. They came upon a large band camped on the North Fork of the San Joaquin, threw burning sticks of wood on their tents and as the Indians ran out, riddled

them with a fusillade of shots. Twenty-four, including the chief, were shot.

While this ended Indian forays temporarily, the governor sent Savage and the Mariposa Battalion into the high Sierra to track down any remaining Indians. One of the last of the scattered bands rounded up was hidden in the mountain valley later known as Yosemite and this ended the Indian episodes of Mariposa. The miners now settled down to work.

The jail at Mariposa, still standing, is built of dressed granite blocks from Mormon Bar, two miles south, mined from an intrusion which is the barrier terminating the Mother Lode on the south. Thus Mariposa becomes the end link in the "Golden Chain" stretching northward along Highway 49. Its history goes back some time before the discovery of gold at Coloma.

The first of several enormous land grants, one that was to effect the current of events for Mariposa, was handed out in 1844 by the Mexican Governor of California, Micheltorena. The recipient was Juan Batista Alvarado who, in August of 1849, sold out to John C. Fremont. This was eighteen months after James Marshall found those yellow flakes in the millrace of his sawmill. The original location of the grant was somewhere at the edge of the San Joaquin Valley but by a convenient and accepted process of the day the grant was "floated" to the Mother Lode country when the value of that area began to boom. This was accomplished merely by shifting the boundaries of the grant, which included 44,000 acres of land.

Mariposa Creek runs between "benches," more or less level, about the width of a city block and narrower. As a natural consequence of the panning and placering the town was laid out along the banks and composed entirely of tents, shacks and a few jerry-built frame buildings. When these got in the way of the creek workings a more substantial town was built on higher, drier ground nearby.

Hard rock mining followed close on the heels of the placering operations in Mariposa Creek, although at first this consisted of little more than scraping off the crumbly, gold-bearing quartz from the tops of the veins and running it through Mexican style arrastres. Kit Carson and two of his companions had found the Mariposa Mine as early as 1849, and by July of that year the production had already outgrown the capacities of the primitive method of crushing. Palmer, Cook and Co. built one of the first stamp mills to handle the ore from the Mariposa Mine and were in full operation by '59.

All this time Fremont was fighting not only these "interlopers" but the owners of the Pine Tree, Josephine and Princeton and many smaller workings. He had no legal recourse under American law until he won his long battle in the courts and was given title to the Las Mariposa grant. He then unceremoniously ousted the erstwhile owners of these mines and reaped the harvest of their investments.

The golden years for the Mariposa Mine were from 1900 to 1915. Total production was estimated at $2,193,205. The shaft did not go straight down but inclined at about 60° and penetrated the lode a distance of 1550 feet. Signs of the mine workings may still be seen a mile south of Mariposa.

SCHLAGETER HOTEL built of brick and wood, has wide wooden balconies. Other old buildings in Mariposa are variously built of granite, soapstone from hills immediately east of town. Soapstone blocks are set in mud mortar on inside wall where weathering is negligible. Other interesting original buildings are Trabuco warehouse, present Bank of America, I.O.O.F. Lodge, Butterfly grocery and the jail.

ERECTED 1854.

MARIPOSA COUNTY
COURT HOUSE

MARIPOSA COUNTY COURT HOUSE is oldest one still in use in California. Front section, original part, was completed in 1854 at a cost of $12,000. Lumber was whipsawed from trees growing nearby, framework fastened with mortised joints and wooden pegs. Finished lumber was hand-planed, nailed with hand-forged square-cut nails. Fire-proof brick vault for safe keeping of records was added in '61, later enlarged. English-made clock with 267 pound bell was installed 1866, has chimed the hours ever since, musically struck five as picture was being made. Court room was scene of many legal battles, has remained exactly the same, with all original furnishings in place.

BEAR VALLEY, CALIFORNIA

Col. John C. Fremont was no man for hard work but he knew what his head was for. When he shifted the boundaries of his 44,000-acre grant to cover the newly discovered gold country from Mariposa to the Merced River, he was very successful in getting others to work the extensive and rich placers on his claim. The many experienced Mexican miners in the area who were unwilling to work for wages were given a grubstake and "share" in a claim along the stream. On this basis they would wade into the water and slosh a pan or shovel gravel into a Long Tom like everybody else.

When the placer workings were going good, Fremont discovered the veins scattering loose gold into the creek bed. In 1851 he started hard rock mining in the lode itself and built several stamp mills to crush the ore. Of his operations he favored those at Bear Valley, first called Simpsonville, and decided to build his home here. It was an imposing structure, called "The White House" by the people in the settlement.

A building boom now set in. Fremont's enterprises erected an elaborate two-story wooden structure with wide, gingerbread balconies, the lumber brought around the Horn in 1850. The hostelry served as headquarters for the Fremont Company and shelter for travelers including Ulysses S. Grant, its formal name being Oso House. Also going up in this period were a number of saloons, a large livery stable and several stores including the huge general mercantile business of the company.

In 1858 Fremont brought to "The White House" his wife, Jessie Benton Fremont, and the children. In June of that year the famous "Mariposa War" came to a head, threatening for a time the lives of the little family. But Col. Fremont was above all a soldier and had seen trouble coming. He had been fortifying his best-known mine, the Pine Tree, against attack by men of the Merced Mining Co., which firm had taken over two other units of the Colonel's properties by force.

The Merced men surrounded the Pine Tree and prepared to stage a seige. Fremont was wily enough to slip a rider through the solid line

ADOBE STORE BUILDINGS are melting away. This is rear section of walls facing street. Door at left opened into establishment of Nicholas Pendola, an Italian who built structure in 1850. Pendola was expert bootmaker, doing repair work as well. Most prominent customer was Col. Fremont himself who had all his boots made here. Iron doors, shipped around Horn are still in place, $800 for the pair. Walls have unusual construction, adobe courses are alternated with schist slabs, quarried in neighborhood. Garbarino Store, General Merchandise adjoins at right.

around the mine who carried a message to the Governor, a desperate plea for help. This was answered in five days by a detachment of state troops which forced both sides to break up, the belligerents were admonished when maneuvered into court.

In 1859 the Supreme Court confirmed Fremont's title and the Mariposa War was officially ended. Later that year Horace Greeley visited Bear Valley, reporting: "The Colonel is now operating two stamp mills and netting $100,000 a year." Whatever the amount, Col. Fremont decided in 1863 it was not worth more gray hairs and sold the entire grant for $6 million. He came out considerably ahead since the original price in '47 was $3,000.

Bear Valley is a ghostly place now. Fremont's fine hotel with its balconies and pillars is gone, set on fire in 1938 by careless campers. Gone also is "The White House." Remaining are many ruined adobe buildings, several schist structures including the roofless jail and a few false fronts on the main street that breathe the atmosphere of the days when Fremont "owned" the town of 3,000 people.

ROOFLESS JAIL stands near schoolhouse on hillside. Built solidly of schist rock set firmly in mortar, structure would seem escape-proof, but further restraint was secured by fastening prisoner by leg-irons to heavy ring of iron in center of floor—common practice when town flourished. Hill behind jail is sparsely forested with digger pines.

HORNITOS, CALIFORNIA

The origin of Hornitos is clouded in doubt. While the gold rush had a violent impact on the sleepy little village it was not the cause of its birth as in the case of most of the towns along the Mother Lode. The Mexican settlement was many years pre-gold rush, built around a central plaza in approved Spanish style, the adobe buildings low and sprawling. A main street ran beside the plaza and formed one side of the square. In the evenings the strumming of guitars issued from the doorways and gay, though decorous, dances were in sway almost every night—*bailles* that included Las Chapanecas, Fandangos and all the rest. Daytimes saw the Mexican sports—bull fights, bull and bear contests and long-legged fighting cocks pitted against each other. Saints days and fiestas were observed, mass celebrated in the small adobe church.

TUNNEL ONCE RAN UNDER STREET from a d o b e which stood in area shown in foreground. Other end was in saloon across street. On one occasion when "Most notorious bandit in California" was surprised by posse at door of Fandango Hall, he ducked into opening shown here and escaped from pursuers. State soon offered $5,000 for his capture, resulting in Murieta's ambush and killing at the mouth of Arroyo Cantova near Priest Valley by a posse of 20 State Rangers headed by Capt. Harry Love in July of 1853.
Murieta's head was severed and the problem arose as to how to preserve it as proof of the slaying. Capt. Love gathered all bottles of whiskey carried by the men which amounted to a total of three quarts. Paste of flour and whiskey was then smeared over grisly object and it was put in a keg, later being taken to a doctor who cleaned it off and more properly preserved it in alcohol. Head was then brought to Hornitos where Murieta had been so well known and lifted out by hair for identification by erstwhile drinking cronies. After this it was placed in glass jar and displayed all over California.

CHINESE "TREES OF HEAVEN" persist from oriental occupation, grow inside ruins of Ghirardelli store. In 1855 Ghirardelli, who previously had operated a trading post on the Stanislaus River, heard of the boom in Hornitos and felt it would be a good place to start a general supply house. Store was built by him and operated three years, when he moved to San Francisco and devoted himself to chocolate business. Upper floor was added to store and used as I.O.O.F. Hall, then as place to hold dances and meetings until demise of town.

EARLIEST BURIALS IN MEXICAN HORNITOS were unusual. Body was placed in simple coffin of boards covered with black cotton cloth lined white. This was placed on top of ground and "tomb" of rock and adobe built up around it. Resemblance to early day bake ovens, called "Hornitos," led to naming of town. Hundreds of these unique above-ground graves were scattered on slope of hill above church, only a few remaining.

BURIAL YARD of Catholic Church is heavily populated, casualties in early days many as result of "miner's consumption," frequent quarrels and violence in bordellos and opium dens. Cemetery has many plots with unique ways of arranging graves and stones. Here graves are covered by walk of stone and cement.

The gold rush changed all this. A gold camp called Quartzburg had sprung up not far away and was running in such wide-open fashion with murders rampant that the peaceful element forcibly ejected the prostitutes, gamblers and troublemakers. Hornitos being handy, these undesirables settled there, disrupting the idyllic course of the town's history. It was written: "Gamblers, girls and roughnecks . . . they were a tough lot, the worst in the southern mines. They reverenced nothing but money, cards and wine . . . blood was upon nearly every doorstep and the sand was caked in it." It was during this period the notorious bandit, Joaquin Murieta, moved in and made as permanent a residence as he did anywhere in his unstable wanderings.

Almost every town in the Mother Lode was said to have been his "hide-out." Some historians have tried to destroy the Murieta legend but facts show there were several Mexican bandits during the period, three named Joaquin—two of these, Joaquin Valenzuelo and Joaquin Carrillo. Blame for the deeds of all was placed on Murieta even though two murders laid at his feet may have been perpetrated many miles apart. It is said Capt. Love and his Rangers were out for a reward and any Mexican would do as a means of collecting the money. It is also reported Murieta's sister made a trip to San Francisco to view the head of her famous brother. If she paid her dollar like other curious spectators she may have felt cheated, as she retorted: "This is not the head of my brother." No one ever claimed to have seen Joaquin Murieta alive after May, 1853.

Gold was plentiful around Hornitos although strictly speaking, the town was about fifteen miles from the Mother Lode proper. Caught with gold fever, the place grew even wilder and the usual entry of Chinese aggravated the situation. The Orientals were the very symbol of peace but they infuriated the whites by their willingness to work for so little on such a low standard of living.

One of these Cantonese was patiently gleaning the leavings of white miners in the gulch one day when a gang of white boys came along to torment him. After taking all this meekly for some time Charley bristled at a particularly mean jibe and fired his gun into the air to scare the boys. The bullet hit a rock and angled into one of his annoyers, inflicting a skin wound. The boy ran home bawling and the resulting hue and cry was so loud Charley tried to run out of town. He was caught and clapped into the tiny jail.

In the middle of the hoosegow floor was (and still is) a short length of heavy chain attached to an iron ring. Ordinarily a rustler or horse thief made no more than a one night stay and to keep him safe, the ring was put over leg irons which were welded together, usually burning the culprit's leg. In the morning, after a quick "trial," he was taken out and hanged.

SLEEPY MAIN STREET shows gap in center where plaza is situated. Building at left was built of adobe and stone in 1852, was originally saloon, ten years later put to use as Masonic Hall, Lodge No. 98. It is said to be the only such hall where meetings are held on the ground floor.

MEXICAN-STYLE PLAZA is at extreme left, old Pacific Saloon at corner. Of simple adobe construction when erected in 1851, it was rendezvous of large cliques of French miners. Purchased in 1862 by Samuel McClatchy, saloon was "dolled up" by removal of old canopy, addition of brick trim around door. Result was so elegant, miners called it "The Bank." Next is thick walled adobe originally built by Mexicans as general store. Merchandise was piled on sidewalk during day where customers pawed over it. In 1860 Mrs. Marck arrived in town from France, bought building for bakery, sold such unlikely items as French pastry which had wide popularity in area.

For some reason, the Chinaman was allowed the freedom of the cell and late that night when he was craving his pipe, he heard voices outside and cringed against the opposite wall. The white men seemed friendly, chatting with him, telling him it was all a big joke and he would be released in the morning. In the meantime they would put his pipe and some tobacco on the ledge of the small window where he could reach it.

When the voices stopped Charley eagerly stepped up on the edge of the bunk to get at the high window. As he reached, his wrist was gripped and he was dragged closer, a noose slipped around his neck. Then several hands took hold of the rope, yanking him against the stone wall of the jail and letting him fall to the floor. This they kept up long after he was killed. None of the gang was ever punished. "It was good enough for the damn Chinks," was the popular opinion.

In spite of constant persecution, the Chinese for a time constituted a major element in the population of Hornitos. Their collection of hovels constructed of odds and ends was located just north of the original Mexican plaza. It was a fantastic labyrinth of basement opium dens with a ground level roof, stores made of packing cases, and some solid adobes. These latter gradually replaced the more flimsy structures and were built above the first "basement" establishments. Several of these remain today, being the first buildings to greet the visitor as he enters the village. The opium den was fitted up in approved fashion, bunks solidly lining the walls. A small opening near the ceiling allowed some of the stale fumes to escape. Here came not only the Orientals but many a white miner who had become addicted to the poppy.

Hornitos had passed through the original phase, the Mexican occupation with its fiestas, the Chinese influx with attendant racial clashes, and now came a new and more peaceful phase. The quartz gold deposits at Quartzburg so rich at first gave out. The white population moved over into Hornitos where the deposits were still productive. These people demanded a measure of law and order, and from then on, children played safely in the streets again.

CATHOLIC CHURCH in center of old burial ground is maintained in good condition, occasional Masses still observed in venerable structure. Note stone buttresses.

LITTLE STREAM WAS FILLED with miners panning the gravels in earliest days of gold rush. In '50s Chinese coolies were employed by hundreds to build stone walls to contain stock on hillsides at 25 cents a day. Remains of these fences extend for miles around Hornitos.

COULTERVILLE, CALIFORNIA

In spite of the hordes of Chinese and Mexicans in the town, the name Coulterville prevailed. It was originally called Banderita and there are two differing versions explaining the use of the name which signifies "little flag" or "bandana" in Spanish.

When the first whites, who of necessity spoke practical Spanish, arrived in the area they found a goodly number of Mexicans already hard at work. Most of the laborers were wearing small bandanas. In another story when George Coulter left his trading post on the Merced River in 1850 and set up shop on Maxwell Creek, site of the fabulous new "diggin's," he hoisted the only avail-

able American flag—a small one--over his tent. The Mexicans took it for the familiar square of colored neck cloth and named the camp Banderita.

The name was of short duration. Coulter's activities were so numerous and varied that his name seemed logical for the town and Coulterville it became. The original Mexican-style plaza, surrounded by nondescript brush "ramadas" and adobes, was maintained but soon outlined with substantial stone and permanent adobes. The influx of more than a thousand Chinese was responsible for many of the latter, this frugal race choosing adobe and rammed earth as being the most economical.

SUBSTANTIAL BUILDING is one of those replacing brush *ramadas* of earlier Mexican occupation. Completed in 1851 it was the second stone and adobe building in Coulterville and among the first in Mother Lode. Built for the Gazolla Store, it was subsequently used as saloon, fandango hall, restaurant and hotel. Ancient umbrella trees, recently beheaded, shade sidewalk.

The first of the pigtails had appeared as early as 1850, establishing a little settlement at the north edge of town. There were the usual twisted streets and opium dives coupled with the inevitable joss house and public bake ovens. These last were built of brick and mortar or mud and were centers for gossip and scandalizing when housewives gathered to do their baking.

Along with the Chinese and half as many Mexicans, there were three thousand American miners and their hangers-on to swell the population of the wildly booming gold camp. The Americans left the placer operations to the foreigners and took to the immediate hillsides to establish the fabulously rich hard rock mines, notably the Mary Harrison. This mine was discovered around 1867 and operated more or less continuously until closed permanently in 1903, after being worked to a depth of 1200 feet by shaft and winch.

The whole area is rich in fine rock, mineral specimens and outcropping, and produces Mari-posite, named for the county. The technical name for the blue-green banded material is chrome mica and it is available everywhere locally. Collectors find white quartz and carbonate minerals such as dolomite, ankerite and calcite. The gold bearing ore consisted of iron pyrites, usually somewhat oxidized.

One completely unorthodox "gold rush" assumed a comic opera aspect, taking place in the middle of the town at the turn of the century. Fire in 1899 destroyed many of the structures. One of the gutted stone buildings was demolished and the rubble shoveled into holes and ruts of the muddy street. A substantial cache of gold, concealed in the wrecked building, was this way buried in the street undetected but the first heavy rain exposed a number of gold coins and nuggets. Almost the entire population turned out to flail the street with shovels and any tool available, leaving it a shambles.

TINY STEAM LOCOMOTIVE was used to haul ore from Mary Harrison mine. Stretch of track was four miles in length, famous as the "World's crookedest railroad." Branches at left are part of Coulterville's "Hang Tree." Dawn of March 16, 1856 saw body of Leon Ruiz dangling from limb. Ruiz was thus punished for slaying of two Chinese miners at Bear Valley and robbing their sluice of gold dust and nuggets worth six hundred dollars. Old oak saw long series of lynchings and "lawful executions."

BIG OAK FLAT, CALIFORNIA

White women were scarce in the early days of the West and particularly during the first several years of California's gold rush. So it was natural for a lonely white miner to take an Indian wife, not necessarily in legal fashion. James Savage—the same Savage who explored the Yosemite Valley while the head of a party pursuing renegade Indians—is assigned a vast loneliness, for he took five aboriginal wives to his bosom. And more, he retained most of their relatives as servants and laborers.

Savage was prospecting the gulches between Deer Creek and Moccasin Creek in 1849 and he and his retinue camped one night under an enormous oak tree on a wide flat. Next morning found the party panning the gravels of the creek and the showings convinced the leader that here they would stay. News of this kind could not be muffled and in a few months hordes of the gold-hungry, disappointed elsewhere, moved into "Savage's Diggings."

Before it was all over the placers of the immediate area had yielded a total of more than $25 million—one of the richest diggings of the Mother Lode. The name of the spot was changed to Big

Oak Flat in honor of the gnarled patriarch standing alone on the only level part of the camp. The tree was of dimensions out of all proportion to other oaks of the mountains and was thought to be the largest in California, with a diameter of thirteen feet at the base, eleven at a man's head.

The oak was still monarch of the flat when the town grew to 3,000 but was succumbing to a man-made cancer. The miners could not resist the temptation to dig closer and closer to the roots until many branches died. Fire in 1862 which destroyed most of the frame buildings caught the dried or dead limbs and finished the life of the old tree. Unrestrained digging around its base at last toppled it in '69 and in 1901 a fire was set against it, burning most of the trunk and all the limbs.

In 1932 the Boys' Service Club of Union High School in Sonoma gathered the remaining fragments of the old oak and built a monument over them beside the road. In a few years this memorial was so decimated by the hackings of vandals that it was necessary to protect them with iron grillwork.

BIG GENERAL MERCANTILE is one of the finest examples of architecture in entire Mother Lode country and one of the best preserved. Built of dressed schist slabs set in lime mortar, the door frames are made square by the use of bricks. Heavy iron doors, characteristic of gold rush style, were shipped around Horn, had bars and hasp inside for securing at night. Not only did doors afford protection against bandits but kept fire out, or contained within.

CHINESE CAMP, CALIFORNIA

It was a fantastic battle—a Pigtail Waterloo. Nine hundred members of the Yan-Wo Tong were pitted against twelve hundred of the Sam Yaps and it was fought with farm tools and venom. And when the air was cleared of yells, the sounds of cymbals and firecracker smoke, the marshals hauled four men to the morgue, two hundred and fifty to the little adobe jails.

The big Tong melee took place in the Mother Lode country before the Civil War. In the preponderantly Chinese population of the camp were several Tong factions, always ready to quarrel with each other. Two of the groups were composed of miners working claims along the Stanislaus River at Two Mile Bar. One claim was held by Celestials belonging to twelve members of the Sam Yap, be-

low it another operated by six brothers of Yan Wo.

A large boulder was dislodged on the upper level and rolled down into the camp below, hurting no one but sparking an argument. The only way to settle it, the powers decided, was by formal battle. And this was not a thing to be undertaken lightly. It required thought and judgment, however miscast. Several American blacksmiths of the town were called upon to make the proper weapons for opposing factions to use with dignity and honor, and into the forges went hundreds of hoes, rakes and whatever could be snatched up from the creek bed and farms.

On Sept. 26, 1856 the Yan Wo horde, mostly from Chinese Camp, clashed on the rocky flat with the defending host of Sam Yaps, hailing generally from

ST. FRANCIS XAVIER CATHOLIC CHURCH built in 1855 by popular subscription of funds and labor, was first regular house of worship in Chinese Camp. Even after church was established with Henry Aleric as first Pastor, miners worked at claims as usual on Sundays and the faithful attended service, piling shovels, pans and outer clothing outside door. Structure originally had shingled roof with belfry and small steeple surmounted by cross. By 1949 it had deteriorated badly and steeple was removed, leaking roof covered with sheet iron and several coats of paint. Cross was then replaced at apex of roof.
Pine in background is of comparatively rare species — *Pinus Sabiniana*. Digger Pine is fairly common on lower slopes of California foothills, has dropping grayish needles, uniquely branched trunk, is somewhat tender.

the nearby camp of Crimea House. As the lines drew close, several contraband firearms were found in both groups. No Chinese were supposed to have them, the law said, but in this case the firing was only spasmodic and did little harm. The fighting consisted mainly of noisy clatter, high-pitched yelling and beating of gongs. Since no important event could take place among Chinese without firecrackers, the smoke and popping of these was added to the general confusion.

Just about the time the going was hot and heavy, four American law officers rode in and stopped the proceedings, arresting a small mob of sweating contestants. Four Tong men lay on the ground and did not move, dead of stab wounds, and four others more or less seriously slashed. The Tong War of Chinese Camp had passed into history.

How so many Chinese came to be together at these diggings is not entirely clear. The several versions are no doubt partly true and each episode contributed to the total of some five thousand. One legend has a group of Englishmen arriving in 1849 to make their fortunes in the undeniably rich placer gravels along the Stanislaus. They discovered however that this would take considerable physical labor and to avoid this they made "raids" on several

OLD STORE has been converted to post office with gabbro cobblestones set in mortar and faced with brick. Outside lock boxes are for convenience of few remaining residents but most patrons go inside to pass time of day with postmaster. Plaque on corner of building honors Eddie Webb, born 1880 in Snelling, California, who was "last of the old-time stage drivers." He hauled freight, passengers and mail from Chinese Camp to Coulterville and Groveland. From 1898 to 1902 he drove the first stage over the new Shawmutt Road.

WHEREVER CHINESE MINERS LIVED they planted *ailanthus* — "Tree of Heaven." Trees are very self-sufficient, have persisted and multiplied until they appear native. Photographer made record of Mother Lode buildings in early spring before appearance of foliage which obscures everything behind it.

neighboring mining camps, offering the Chinese workers more money than they had been getting. Altogether they lured away several hundred workers to operate the long toms—enlarged and more elaborate than the rockers in general use after the first simple pan workings.

Then it was said there was the ship's captain who deserted his vessel in San Francisco and headed for the diggings, bringing the entire Chinese crew with him to do the pick and shovel work. Some say the two gangs worked toward each other and when they met, formed and named the town. If this is to be believed, the yellow men must have been members of the same Tong.

In any event the usual evidences of the early day gold camp sprang up—stores, banks, livery stables, honky tonks and brothels. There were enough whites and Mexicans intermixed with the Orientals to erect a fine Catholic church, as well as hotel, Masonic and Sons of Temperance lodges and Wells Fargo Express office. An organization was formed to bring water to the mines, solving the problem by building an elaborate flume from Wood's Creek.

Today most of the buildings and all the Chinese are gone but plenty of relics remain to give the visitor a picture of what life was like in those hectic days of the gold rush.

JAMESTOWN, CALIFORNIA

The gold discovery at Sutter's Mill changed the course of history for the state and in a degree for the entire West. But the "rush" was a walk rather than a headlong plunge. Easterners were slow to hear the tidings and when they first came it was by slow boat around the Horn. But even these got to the Sierra foothills ahead of the ones who came across country by wagon.

So it was the opportunists already on the Coast who got to the gold first and had the choice of the best localities. One of the early birds was Col. George F. James and although his stint at mining was short, his name is bright in the memories of one of the picturesque Mother Lode towns.

When the big story broke Col. James was a resident of San Francisco and he was curious to know how much of the talk was true. He had never liked his staid legal profession and was ready to make a switch to adventure. Rumor said it was impossible to get tools at the diggings so he bought what he thought he would need in San Francisco at "hold up" prices. Sellers of pan, shovel and pick were gouging customers with a flourish and prices of salt pork, dried beef, beans, flour and rice had doubled and tripled. James also laid in a few do-it-yourself remedies such as calomel, "blue pills," quinine and laudanum since doctors were almost unknown in the camps and these few, mostly quacks.

James headed for the hills, first by wagon, then horse and finally on foot. He followed the lead of the discoveries at Wood's Crossing, taking samples in each stream he crossed. In the shadow of Table Mountain, about four miles southwest of where Sonora would soon be established, he decided to camp a while.

"Sonora Road" camps sprang up, "thick as hair on a dog's back—Cloudmans, Chinese Camp, Montezuma, Yorktown, Curtisville, Sullivan's Green Springs, Camp Seco and Hardtack.

The gravels of Wood's Creek were rich and James's camp grew to be christened Jamestown.

OLD EMPORIUM has been doing business as usual since Gay Nineties and remains virtually unchanged. Aged Chinaman ambles down street redolent of the days when his countrymen scrambled over tailings to harvest meager crumbs of gold left by careless white men. Many buildings in today's Jamestown retain vintage charm, although town is not a bonafide "ghost," being one of several links in the Golden Chain along Highway 49 which have stayed active after the wild days.

BRANCH JAIL was used again in World War I days, later as home for owner, then abandoned. Brick of construction is typical but cast stone uncommon in Mother Lode. Several cement plants were operated in later years where limestone lenses offered suitable material as in areas along Calaveras Creek, southeast and southwest of San Andreas. Some deposits are dolomitic with too high a magnesia content for good cement.

CURIOUS SHEEP stops to watch photographer make picture of abandoned gateway to old cabin in back street of Jamestown. Mailbox and ancient grapevine are mute evidence of past human habitation.

Jamestown prospered but James did not. He couldn't get along with the other men, partly because so many of them were rougher than his former law associates and partly because he wanted to be boss and these hardy individuals would not stand still for orders. When James departed the diggings in a rage one day he walked right out of the history of the town he founded.

But the memory of the man lingered on and the miners wanted no more of it, changing the name Jamestown to American Camp. This title lasted long enough for tempers to cool, but back came Jamestown, and more familiarly—Jimtown.

One of the best known workings of the James-town area was begun in 1856 when James App and his party became interested in a promising vein on Quartz Mountain. When the mine began to pay off and App felt he could afford to marry, he chose Leanna Donner for his mate. Leanna was one of the six children who had lost their parents in the tragedy at Donner Pass. She outlived her husband by many years, reaching the age of 95. She died on the old App homestead in 1930.

Jamestown today is not a dead ghost but retains much of the charm of its early roistering days even though there are cars parked along the main street and the old buildings are somewhat disguised by modern signs and electric lights.

SONORA, CALIFORNIA

The story of the gold camp with the musically pleasant name, Sonora, is a story of race discrimination and riot. It was a hell roaring boom town with a polyglot population, the dregs of a dozen races. Called Sonoran Camp by the Mexicans who were the sole and peaceful occupants for several years, it was quickly changed to Sonora, as the peace was changed to violence—by the Americans.

Both Sonora and Jamestown were brought into being by gold discoveries along Wood's Crossing by a party headed by Rev. James Woods, and including James Savage, J. H. Rider and Charles Bassett. The richness of the gravel deposits in the stream was almost unbelievable and the men set to work with feverish energy, and were for some time able to extract about $250 a day by the simplest means. This surface bonanza persisted for several years and the camp called Wood's Crossing was a flourishing, hell-bent settlement.

In less than a year there were more than 2,000 people in camp—an unholy assemblage of Mexicans, Chileans, Chinese and Americans. By the fall of '49 there were 5,000. Shanties had been so hastily thrown up so close together, the narrow

ST. JAMES EPISCOPAL CHURCH, most outstanding old building in Sonora. On "Piety Hill" with four other churches, it survived several fires which devastated most frame buildings at various times. Construction was started in 1859 on a site donated by Caleb Dorsey. Funds for building materials were also donated to finish building the same year. Architect was the Rev. John Gassman of San Francisco who also served as first minister. Beautiful structure stands at head of Washington, the main street, and dominates Queen of the Southern Mines.

Less than a hundred yards from church, also in heart of town is Big Bonanza mine. First worked in 1851 by Chileans who took large amounts of surface gold from the spot, claim was later purchased by three partners for small sum. They operated mine conservatively for three years, then suddenly broke into a solid pocket of gold. Next day they shipped $160,000 worth to the San Francisco mint. During the next week they took out half a million, and another before they sold out.

streets could hardly contain the traffic and were almost impassable on Sundays when everybody was "in town."

The lowest elements flocked to Sonora and violence quickly broke out, murders and street shootings being everyday occurrences. A miners' meeting was held and R. S. Ham selected as alcalde. Some semblance of law and order was achieved but trouble continued to brew in the gambling dives, brothels and opium dens. Although a large portion of the trouble makers were Americans from San Francisco at first, later from the East, the blame fell on the minority groups.

The Americans had gained confidence by the outcome of the Mexican War and being already convinced of their natural supremacy, called the others "foreigners." They decided to get rid of the Mexicans and Chileans but tolerate the Chinese who had proven useful in menial capacities. Under a program of steady abuse, many Mexicans gave up and meekly left their claims for healthier climates but others banded together and rebelled to the point of making guerilla warfare against the Americans, staging skirmishes in which twelve murders were perpetrated in a few weeks.

In June of 1850, the legislature passed a law stating that before any foreigner could operate his mine, even though the claim was established before the Americans moved in, he would have to pay a levy of $30. Since most workings were paying well, this amount could easily have been borne by the Mexicans, but the obvious injustice so rankled that further trouble flared. The Mexican miners organized to defy authorities, refused to pay the tax and continued to operate their claims under protection of armed guards.

The situation had by now become so tense everybody went armed and the potential for an explosion needed only a spark. This was soon provided. A party of whites came upon several Mexicans and Indians engaged in a proceeding which made their tempers jump. The dark-skinned suspects had constructed a funeral pyre of logs and on it were the bodies of two Americans, the wood ready for the torch. Such strong circumstantial evidence of murder seemed ample to those who wished it to be and the foreigners were dragged into town and jailed. A howling mob bore down on the little structure and hauled the men to nearest hanging tree. Nooses were slipped around their necks, the bodies actually off the ground when rescue in the form of an armed sheriff's posse arrived. The same posse also rounded up several hundred Mexican "sympathizers" in order to avoid a mass attack in case the accused were convicted of murder.

The town was jammed with miners from all over the area the day of the trial. Just as court was about to convene somebody accidentally fired his gun and another riot was on. Men poured out of the courthouse by every exit on top of those standing outside to listen to the trial. No one knew what had started the commotion or what the trouble was all about but all were willing to fire their guns in all directions and at anything. A huge business done at the saloons before trial was now showing its effects. When the excitement, dust and smoke had settled, it turned out that only feelings had been hurt, with a minor flesh wound or two. The affair served to blow off steam and the trial was conducted in a somewhat more deliberate manner.

The outcome heightened embarrassment still more. The suspects were found to have been conducting funeral services in their own fashion for the two Americans whom they had discovered dead. The prisoners were then turned loose as were those held in corrals for the "duration."

This affair did not end persecution of the Mexicans, on the contrary probably intensifying it. The Mexicans now realized their position was insecure to say the least and when the order for taxes was enforced by armed collectors, they performed a mass exodus from Sonora. This had a result unexpected by the rest of the population. Their town became a near-ghost with more than half the business potential gone, stores falling upon lean days. After a year of virtual famine, the tax laws were repealed. Some of the exiles returned but the best days were gone for Sonora.

"The Queen of the Southern Mines" continued to operate her many shifts and tunnels—developments that had long replaced the surface operations of earlier days. Hard rock mining was more permanent and paid off to a total of $40 million before it was all over. The "Magic Circle" producing all this wealth was only four miles across, with Sonora at its center.

SAWMILL FLATS, CALIFORNIA

Three miles southeast of Columbia, a mile and a half south of Yankee Hill, is a clearing in a once dense forest. The nearly level area is on the banks of Wood's Creek, the same stream that figured so prominently in the histories of Sonora and a dozen other gold camps. Gold however did not bring the swarms of people there in the early 1850s. Here in the center of a bountiful supply of standing timber were established two large sawmills. Lumber was a scarce commodity in the early gold rush days and it brought a good price, creating a boom camp at Sawmill Flat.

At first not many Americans were willing to work in the mills, too many were eager to pan for gold or work for someone who had built a series of Long Toms or was sluicing the beds of the stream. There was always a possibility of pocketing good nuggets while guaranteed a daily wage of $2.50 a day. The first employees at the mills were almost all Peruvians and Mexicans. Being clannish, both races had established "segregated" saloons and stores, nearly every facility in town being duplicated. A population of over a thousand had grown up around the mills when an exciting event was noised around in spite of every effort to suppress it. Only a short distance north of the center of town a good strike of gold had been made.

Yet disappointment was due those who rushed up the creek to stake claims—disappointment and astonishment. The claims were already staked out —and by whom? By no one less than a strikingly beautiful Mexican woman! Her name was Dona Josepha Elisa Martinez and to discourage any too-ardent fortune hunters, she had brought from Mexico a motley crowd of peons, ready to defend their lady boss. The senora was already wealthy and the gravels of Wood's Creek and several shallow surface workings swelled her coffers earlier filled with gems and fancy clothes.

But being wealthy was not enough for the Dona Martinez. She was lonely. So it was opportune that a handsome young Mexican with curly black hair and luxuriant mustache called on her and introduced himself as Joaquin Murieta. He said he was a monte dealer who had fallen into some trouble and would she hide him for a while? Hide him she did and since that all happened before Murieta became notorious, his face familiar to many a victim of robbery and hold-up, he vanished completely from the posse on his trail.

Once he felt safe, he again took the bandit route and soon returned to hide with the lovely senora. This time she was able to conceal him only a short while. His hideout, the first of many to become known, was precarious. Murieta left hurriedly by the back door one night and Josepha Elisa, in her camp now called Martinez, as well as the populace of Sawmill Flats, knew him no more.

In 1857 a disastrous fire almost leveled nearby Columbia, the best customer of the mills. It was the worst but not the first of the fires that destroyed most of the flimsy buildings of the boom town. Columbia ruefully surveyed its ashes and decided that this time rebuilding would be done with brick. This was the death knell for Sawmill Flat and it gently folded. The rich deposits of gold at neighboring Martinez were soon scratched off and that collection of shanties also died, the senora returned to Mexico with her loot and without her swarthy bandit. The camp of Martinez vanished almost from sight and only a few shacks and cabins remained to mark the site of Sawmill Flats.

ONE OF FEW REMAINING CABINS at Sawmill Flats near collapse, with stone foundation and walls probably built of scraps from the sawmills. Ancient grapevine arches over south wall, leaves all but covering structure in summer. Buildings at site were all flimsy, show no sign of stone, adobe or brick walls. This wooden one has survived because high stone foundation kept rot from beams.

COLUMBIA, CALIFORNIA

John Huron Smith decided he needed one more drink to top off his monumental glow. With bad luck he picked a bar owned by the John Barclays of unsavory reputation. Martha Barclay was alone at the bar and refused Smith his drink. In a violent argument Smith gave Martha a hard shove just as Barclay entered. Drawing his pistol, he killed the belligerent Smith.

The whole matter might have ended there as justifiable had the Barclays not been in constant trouble with the authorities. A friend of Smith's, State Senator J. W. Coffroth, took up the affair and incited the people of Columbia to form a mob and take matters into their own hands. They broke into the jail where Barclay was being held and in the dead of night rushed him to the high flume that carried water to the town. A rope was thrown over the timbers, one end knotted around the prisoner's neck. He was jerked off the ground and one man held up a flaming pine torch to see how the victim was making out. Barclay was holding the rope above his head in a desperate grip, his executioners having neglected to tie his hands. It didn't take long for one of the lynchers to beat the hands loose with the butt of a pistol—and Martha was a widow. The early days of Columbia in the Mother Lode were highlighted with stirring episodes like this.

The glitter of rich gold in the gulch at the foot of Columbia's Main Street was exposed by accident. On March 27, 1850, Dr. Thaddeus Hildreath,

his brother George and several other prospectors, reached this point at nightfall and camped under a large tree, with every intention of moving on in the morning. During the night there was a torrential rainstorm which soaked every blanket. The morning was warm and sunny, the blankets spread out to dry and to pass the time the men took their prospecting tools to the gulch to the foot of what was later called Kennebec Hill. Color of such brilliance showed up in the gravels every man in addition to John Walker, who had made the first find, stayed on. In the next two days the men took out thirty pounds of gold worth $4,680.

The resultant rush to "Hildreth's Diggings," later named Columbia, surpassed almost all others in history. Bursting from a population of nothing to a roaring camp of 5,000 gold-starved souls took

OLD WELLS FARGO EXPRESS COMPANY building, best known of remaining structures in Columbia, architectural showpiece of the Southern Mines. Original office was established in American Hotel lobby. When hotel burned it was moved to Fallon House with William Daeger as express agent. Present structure was erected by Daeger in 1857, with grand opening early in '58, builder continuing as agent until '72.

Brick sidewalks laid diamond-fashion was characteristic of times, have escaped fate of similar ones later covered with cement. Lavish use of bricks in Columbia indicates excellent quality of lateriric clays in locality. Two brickyards operated during boom, were situated on old Dambach Ranch in Matelot Gulch, two miles north of Columbia. Marble-like limestone formations laid bare by sluicing were not utilized as building material although marble quarry here shipped cut stones to San Francisco as early as '54. Delicate, lacy wrought iron balcony grilles were shipped around Horn to San Francisco, hauled to Columbia by mule freight.

only a month. Obviously enough permanent buildings to house this host could not be built so quickly and miners slept under every conceivable kind of shelter—or none at all. April is a mild month in the Mother Lode country and many a miner threw a blanket on the ground when the day's digging was done and collapsed in weariness. He slept in his sweat-soaked clothes and worked in them the next day. When even he could no longer stand the aroma of "ripeness", he would put on his other shirt and hang the first one on a branch to freshen. If it was perchance sprinkled with rain, so much the better. If not, he wore it again when the relief shirt became unbearable.

A lady reporter from San Francisco was said to be interviewing the miners about their lives and habits, asking one bearded man digging in the gravel how he did his laundry. Wiping his brow with his sleeve, he told her: "Lady—we don't use much starch."

The hundreds of flimsy frame structures erected were soon destroyed by fire. Brick buildings replaced them but in the next decade many of these were doomed by the discovery that the ground beneath them held a wealth of gold and the metal could be sluiced out. The first building to go was the first put up and the bricks were sold in other camps. By the time the '60s were over half the buildings in town had been demolished and the materials sold in Sonora and Copperopolis. One stately structure was spared, digging ending at the yard of St. Anne's Church.

Sluicing became such a mania owing to the immense pay-off the entire area around the town was soon a boneyard of bare limestone rocks which stand today as mute reminders of the period. Other towns were also washing soil down the creeks until the valleys were choked with silt and farms covered by mud when the water was high. The mass of soil and debris descending from the mountain camps became such a problem that the State Legislature passed laws banning all such sluicing.

During the boom days prices of commodities reached heights undreamed of in California. Sugar brought $3 a pound, molasses $50 a barrel, flour $1.50 a pound and onions $1, sardines and lobsters $4 a can, candles 50c each and the essential miners' knives $30.

TUOLUMNE ENGINE HOUSE. Columbia h a d history of bad fires, worst on July 10, 1854 and in August '57. After latter committee was authorized to purchase fire engine. Arriving in San Francisco, delegation looked at "sample"—hand pumper made for King of Sandwich Islands (now Hawaii). Rig was named Papeete, gaily decorated with paintings of back-bar type damsels and ready to ship. Enamored citizens of Columbia made successful dicker and rig still stands in Columbia fire house with its hoses of cowhide sections riveted together.
Printing office upstairs published two newspapers, *Columbia Gazette* and *Miner's Advertiser*. Bill Steinfeller's Saloon did business on ground floor. At extreme right was "Doc Parson's" drug store, later notorious Pay Ore Saloon.

About 1858 a novel system of furnishing illuminating gas to the town was completed. Large kilns were constructed to roast pitchy pine from the high mountains, the gas carried to houses through wooden pipes. One difficulty after another beset the new company, pipes leaking, the cutting of wood for burning becoming prohibitive in cost. The gas system lasted only a few months and Columbia was back to kerosene lamps, these serving until the advent of electricity at the turn of the century.

The first public high school system began in rented quarters in '54 and six years later moved into its own two-story brick school house. Still standing, the building is one of the oldest schoolhouses in California, classes being held there until 1937.

During Columbia's big, booming years the streets were jammed with traffic. Stage coaches ran on daily schedules. Freight lines operated from Stockton, bringing all sorts of provisions and supplies. The usual gambling rooms, saloons and dance halls were plentiful and houses on the back streets offered their fancy women. An arena was built for a special type of exhibition, fights between bears and bulls.

The contests were advertised as battles between "Wild Bulls from Spain and Savage Grizzlies from the Remote Mountains of California." Often as not the bull was a doltish reject from the Sacramento slaughterhouse and the bear some mangy specimen cornered in the foothills. Usually both animals were interested only in escaping to the free hills and the miners would demand their money back. And even when the bear was gored into a shapeless mass, the miners would still insist on a refund. Horace Greeley, writing about these battles in the New York Tribune is said to have started the use of the terms "bull" and "bear" in relation to the fluctuations of the stock market.

Columbia was needing more and more water for mining as well as domestic use and to meet the demand the Tuolumne Water Company was organized in 1851. It constructed a vast network of reservoirs, ditches and flumes many miles in length. The miners complained the Company was charging excessive rates and needed some competition, and so organized the Stanislaus River Water Company in '54. It's completed aqueduct wound 60 miles through the mountains to Columbia. The project cost over a million dollars and by the time it was finished so were the lush days of Columbia. Surface gold had been virtually exhausted and expensive hardrock mining was under-

COLUMBIA'S LITTLE JAIL was stoutly constructed, had two cells each with opening through which meals were passed to prisoners.

taken reluctantly. The population declined and by 1860 the Tuolumne Company bought out the miners' water works for $125,000.

During its heyday, Columbia had a large Chinatown. This was natural in any West Coast mining town but surprising enough, this one had Italians, French and Irish sections as well as ones called Negro Hill, French Flat, Texas Flat and a neighborhood of Chileans. Most of these sectors were filled with flimsy wooden shacks and as the town began to fade, so did the foreign "ghettos." The same fate befell a double line of cabins extending the whole distance, four miles, to the slightly older town of Sonora. Hardly a sign is left of these shelters. The once sprawling metropolis gradually shrank to its solid nucleus of brick.

But it did not die completely. After the gold rush was over the more substantial buildings did not fall into complete decay nor were they "prettied up" or covered with garish new fronts, as in the case of many of the better preserved towns founded by the Argonauts.

"Recognizing the opportunity to preserve and interpret for future generations a typical Gold Rush town, the state legislature enacted legislation creating Columbia Historic State Park," says a brochure on this Park, "In addition to preserving the remaining historical structures in the main business section of the town, lands are in the pro-cess of being acquired in the surrounding blocks in conformity with a master plan approved by the State Park Commission on Sept. 17, 1948, thus assuring the preservation of outstanding historic sites and providing for an adequate setting for this 'Gem of the Southern Mines.'" Due to this studied program there are no modern signs or neon lights and the buildings, while preserved, do not have a stark, "rehabilitated" look, showing instead the effect of a mellowing with age.

EARLY MORNING LIGHT reaches under ornate balcony of hostelry once known affectionately as "What Cheer House," more formally as Morgan's Hotel and later City Hotel. First building on site was frame structure, bought by George Morgan early in July, '54 and remodeled for saloon and was burned to ground ten days later. In '56 he built the first unit of two-story Ale House and Billiard Saloon, this entirely destroyed by fire in '57. Present brick building contained lodgings, theater, bar and Music Hall upstairs, was still operating as City Hotel until 1930s.

"All at once ... no one was there!"

VALLECITO, CALIFORNIA

The first discovery of gold at the site on Coyote Creek was actually made by John and Daniel Murphy. They were excited by their find and christened the infant camp Murphy's Diggings. But after a few months of panning the stream, the yield fell short of expectations and the brothers moved on to found the bigger camp of Murphy, after which the original location was called "Murphy's Old Diggings." Then the Mexicans drifted in to the Coyote Creek camp and satisfied with smaller amounts of gold dust, established a tiny village which they called Vallecito.

The word is the Spanish equivalent for "a little valley." Any Mexican settlement in such a situation was likely to be so called and there were a good many Vallecitos in California's early days. Only two have survived. One is an old Butterfield Stage station in San Diego county, the other a Gold Rush town in Calaveras county.

In 1850 the Mexicans arranged a little plaza

GILLEADO BUILDING, sole remnant of once boisterous gold town of Douglas Flat, two and a half miles northeast of Vallecito. Constructed in '51 of limestone blocks now stabilized with concrete, was used in several capacities, among them store and bank. At rear is small hole, reputed to be shotgun window for use of guard who watched safe full of gold. Other limestone buildings in Douglas Flat, relics of gold rush days, were torn down for material to build fences.

SHIP'S BELL used to call congregation to church, sound fire alarms, summon children to school, announce funerals and election results. Early in 1854 Vallecito sent delegation to San Francisco where ship had been abandoned when crew headed for gold fields. Ship's bell had been cast in Troy, N. Y. in '53, was purchased and brought to town. Since church had no steeple, bell was mounted nearby in large oak, served through life of Vallecito, then hung silent many years, finally falling to ground when tree blew down in hard wind of Feb. 16, 1939. In October of that year bell was mounted on monument at site by Native Sons of the Golden West. Stump of tree is shown at right. Other stories contradict legend on bronze plaque, insist bell is too large for ship type, not meant to be rung by lanyard connected to clapper.

after the fashion in their home land and put up temporary brush *ramadas* around it. In the next two years a few more substantial adobes were added and life moved along in sleepy siesta fashion.

Suddenly, in the fall of '52, all this was changed. A vein of gold far richer than the stream gravels was found to run more or less through the center of the camp. The Americans moved in and push-ing the original miners out of the way, soon had the plaza plowed up and the buildings razed, establishing another center a block or so away. Saloons went up first, then a miner's hotel, fandango hall and several stores, followed by a bank, express office, school and finally a post office.

After the original burst, Vallecito settled down to a steady existence without much further expansion and had a good period of productivity.

MURPHYS, CALIFORNIA

If it is true there are more Murphys in Ireland than people, it could be there were more bandits in Murphys than Murphys. In so many mining camps the name of the first man to find gold was good enough for the camp's name, and it was this way in the case of Murphys, even after the original Murphy was all but forgotten in furor and fooferaw caused by stage robbers Joaquin Murieta and Black Bart.

When news of the gold strike at Coloma reached brothers Daniel and John Murphy, they dropped their hods of bricks as it were and "broke for the mines" with pals Henry Angel and James Carson, arriving in the Sierra foothills in the spring of 1848.

While the Murphy brothers paused to try their luck at the spot where Vallecito would later develop, their companions went on to establish diggings known as Angel's Camp and Carson Hill. This country looked good to the Murphys too and while Henry Angel was still looking for gold, the luck of the Irish brought it to the Murphys in big dollops. Gold-hungry prospectors came to Murphys' Camp and they had time to speak only one name—Murphys.

It is the remains of a town now, full of gold rush atmosphere. Many of the original buildings are standing with little alteration. The town is also full of legends and stories of the roaring '50s, among them accounts of Joaquin Murieta's start upon his notorious career of banditry. The tale may be fanciful but Murieta would not have been the first Mexican unjustly persecuted by the Americans.

Joaquin and his brother were arrested in Murphys, accused of a robbery they had not even heard of. They were tied to a tree (the little jail now standing just below the main street not yet built), a group of American miners dragged Joaquin's wife out in the street and in full sight of the brothers was gang-raped. The brother was then strung up in the tree and while his body still jerked, Joaquin was brutally flogged. With the warning—"Next time you're caught stealing we'll hang you, too!"—he was released and sent packing.

Barely able to sit on his horse yet inflamed with rage, Joaquin Murieta left town to become a professional desperado. Few towns in the gold hills do not have stories of the bandit's visits.

Murphys can also tell you about Black Bart. Proof exists that he at least "slept here", his own signature still on the register in the old hotel, not once but several times—Charles (or C. E.) Bolton, Silver, Montana.

"Black Bart" began his double-dealing career by robbing a stage in 1875, industriously holding up twenty-eight others in the following eight years. He always worked alone and never left a clue, usually completing the deed with the flourish of a piece of verse, such as this masterpiece with its misspelled words:

> I've labored long and hard for bread
>   for honnor and for riches
> But on my corns to long yove tred
> You fine haired sons of bitches

MITCHLER HOTEL. Side entrance shows construction of rough limestone chunks set in lime mortar. Partners John Perry and G. L. Sperry, of flour fame, put up building in 1855. Register contains many names which became great, signatures of Mark Twain, Horatio Alger, Thomas Lipton, Henry Ward Beecher, the Rothchilds, General U. S. Grant, John Jacob Astor and C. E. Bolton, better known as "Black Bart" who stayed several nights while spending daytime robbing stages.
He is not known to have molested old safe, then in hotel office, which held many thousands in gold dust and nuggets. Typical iron doors and shutters of Mother Lode buildings were impassable. Metal also furnished fire protection, although in one case they confined fire so well heat pressure caused building to explode, scattering flaming embers all over the town.

LOOKING PAST WALL of old Mitchler Hotel, now called Murphys Hotel, at First Congregational Church. First house of worship was Union Church, erected on this site in 1863. Later Congregational group took over building, using it until '95. Total of 30 pastors served here over the years.

The beginning of his end came on November 3, 1885 near San Andreas when he found the strong box on a stage bolted to the floor. He was wounded while trying to watch the driver and rifle the box at the same time. Although he escaped, he dropped his handkerchief identified with his laundry mark. Wells Fargo detectives found him in his San Francisco apartment where he had been living as a respected Charles Bolton the other part of his life. The trial at San Andreas was speedy, expedited by a plea of guilty. Bolton served several years at San Quentin and was never heard of again.

The skilled engineers among Murphy's miners made real accomplishments in a suspension flume conveying water across Murphy's Creek and a drainage system to dry out the flat where the first claim was located. The main business portion of the camp was consumed by fire August 20, 1859, after which a volunteer fire department was organized. Another picturesque group was the Calaveras Light Guards, started for the purpose of recruiting men for the Civil War.

After the creek beds had given up their supply of gold, the soil-removing and sluicing operations were carried on until forced to stop by law. After that, Murphys tamed down but stayed alive. Although the mines in the area were classed as "never sensational," the camp produced some $20 million.

ALTAVILLE, CALIFORNIA

The question is: Does Altaville owe its place in history to the producing of its gold or its fossilized relic? For here, down 130 feet in the Matison Mine, was found the "Calaveras Skull," subject of controversy and confusion.

When gold in the Mother Lode's easily worked placer streams began to run thin in 1850, miners found more of it in gravel beds above and then in ancient deposits far below the level of active stream beds. This was mighty old gold, as evidenced by the fossil leaves and riffles found with it. Near Altaville several drift mines were developed with shafts as deep as 300 feet.

The Matison Mine was one of these and the finding of the old skull put the Mother Lode in the news more than the gold did. Scientists saw irrefutable proof that man was far more ancient than formerly believed, the public laughed at it as a gigantic hoax and Prof. J. D. Whitney became the man of the hour.

Out of the tangled web of tales about the skull finding is the clear fact that this gentleman, then State Geologist, in January of 1866, had exposed a wildcat scheme of a local financier to foist worthless stocks on the people of Altaville. His act made some bitter enemies but their wrath was blunted by the uncovering of the skull "dating back to Pliocene times."

The whole world heard about the discovery that July. At a meeting of the California Academy of Sciences at San Francisco, Prof. Whitney read a paper confirming the authenticity of the Pliocene Skull. From then on for years the press was full of stories on the subject, many scientists eager to accept the age of the relic, others scoffing. One newspaper reported, "The unscientific public hailed the story as a huge joke on the state geologist perpetrated by the fun loving citizens of the camp." Bret Harte covered the subject in one of his later contributions to the "Californian", the poem "To The Pliocene Skull." In 1903 the American Anthropological Society accepted the skull as a genuine relic but questioned the extreme age which admitted the presence of prehistoric caves in the Sierra Nevada.

And for the light touch is the story that about the time the skull was found, Dr. Kelly, nearby Angel's Camp dentist, failed to find something— the skull of his laboratory skeleton.

HEADSTONE in old section of Altaville cemetery which contains many interesting monuments from gold rush days. Unique in shape, headstone memorializes Alfredo Ribero by portrait cemented to marble. Picture remains unfaded through long years of strong sunshine, was made by converting photographic emulsion to enamel then baked on porcelain base. Uniform is likely that of local Militia during Civil War days.

MOKELUMNE HILL, CALIFORNIA

The Oregonians almost didn't make it. The fact that they did was due to the persuasive powers of two members of the party insisting they keep on digging after utter discouragement—and these two were forever blessed. The men were prospecting along the Mokelumne River in October, 1848, the pickings slim, provisions slimmer. Then the rich strike in the river sands and no one wanted to leave. Yet someone had to or they would all starve.

A man named Syrec finally made the break, promising himself to make up for all the wealth he would miss digging, by setting up a trading post. This he did with food, supplies and a tent he brought back from Stockton. He set up for business on a hill near the scene of operations.

The place was called Mokelumne Hill and other kinds of business ventures mushroomed around this first tent store, among them a boarding house, also in a tent. Later structures were more sturdy but in August 1854 fire levelled the camp. Subsequently building was largely of stone and several of these structures have survived.

Mokelumne Hill, during the hectic '50s, "enjoyed" a widespread reputation for wildness based on acts of violence of all sorts. Just south of town is Chili Gulch, scene of the Chilean War fought in December, 1849. This affair started over the prac-

MAYER BUILDING erected in 1854, showing beautifully tooled construction, Mokelumne Hill being blessed with local supply of light brown rhyolite tuff. Interior of one-time saloon is filled with "Trees of Heaven," evidences of Chinese population from several hundred to two thousand. At height of Oriental influx there were three joss houses and a "slave market" where young Chinese girls were put on the block.

tice of some mine owners, a Dr. Concha among them, of taking claims in the names of their peon help. Since claims were so rich they were limited to sixteen square feet, often yielding hundreds of dollars a day, American miners bitterly resented the Chilean method of acquiring extra claims. They passed stringent laws against the practice but Dr. Concha led a party of men into a gulch occupied by Americans who had dispossessed him and drove them out with several fatalities. The diplomatic dispute between the United States and Chile which followed was finally settled in favor of the Americans.

In the town itself, during a period of seventeen weeks, as many men were killed in arguments and fights. Then after a period of comparative calm, five more men met violent deaths one week end.

The French War was about as one-sided as any fracas could be. A group of French miners had made a fine strike on a small hill they called "French Hill" and in a burst of pride raised the Tricolor over their camp. Americans claimed this was an insult to their flag, stormed the hill, drove the Frenchies out and took over their claims.

Many other tales are told about life in Mokelumne Hill. There is a waggish one about a negro who entered the camp and innocently asked help in locating a claim. Jokers sent him to an area repeatedly prospected without success. The negro started to dig dutifully. Nothing was heard of him for several days until he came back to thank his benefactors. His bag was full of gold nuggets. Before he could return to the claim, the whites had swarmed in.

There is the Joaquin Murieta legend without which no Mother Lode town would be complete. A young miner named Jack, flushed with gold and whiskey, was playing poker with his cronies when the popular subject of the Mexican desperado came up. Jumping up on the table Jack loudly proclaimed: "I've got $500 here that says I'll kill the———the first time I come face to face with him!" This was the signal for a Mexican, unnoticed till now, to stand up and say: "I'll take that bet." In one swoop he grabbed the poke Jack was recklessly displaying and made for the door, vanishing in the dust of his horse's hoofs. Murieta, of course, in one of his more playful moments.

While American miners objected violently to the peon system of mining, claiming "slave la-

OLD CEMETERY in Mokelumne Hill is sombre with grove of Italian cypress, macabre effect heightened by flock of vultures wheeling overhead at dusk, seeking roosting places in trees.

bor" they condoned another and more vicious form of slave traffic. During the height of the gold rush and before women flocked to the camps, any female willing to share her bed with a lonely miner was worth hard cash, with few questions asked about color or race.

To fill this demand enterprising ship owners in San Francisco bought Chinese girls from poverty stricken parents in Canton and other Oriental ports, loaded them on ships under indescribably filthy conditions and brought them to San Francisco for distribution to the gold camps. Mokelumne Hill's big Chinatown was one outlet for the girls, sold outright to miners or housed in shacks and "rented out." Later the more aggressive white prostitutes crowded them out. The Oriental waifs returning to San Francisco to supply its burgeoning Chinese colony.

JACKSON, CALIFORNIA

As a ghost, Jackson is lively. It was never rich in diggings but prospered from the swarm of smaller camps surrounding it and as a stopping place for miners on their way to them. Many of those camps have vanished from the earth, some leave a few visible remnants of gold rush history.

Butte City, with its gaunt stone Ginnochio Store, once operated by a Sr. Bruno, is one. Then there is Bedbug, so called by the first miners there. When the gold supply grew scant and settlers raised cattle, they considered the name too inelegant and substituted Freezeout. A few years went by and this name fell to the more romantic one of Ione, after a lady character in Bulwer-Lytton's "Last Days of Pompeii." This name lived and so did Ione, but Shirttail could not last out, leaving only the name to wonder about. It seems a party of prospectors came upon a lone miner's camp. Considering himself alone in the world, he was standing in the stream sloshing his pan in circles and for convenience in this wet work, he wore only a shirt.

Muletown was a stirring little place in the '50s but only yarns about it remain. In one of these a newly arrived Chinaman picked up a piece of gold weighing thirty-six ounces and was so excited he immediately returned to his homeland. Scottsburg had its historic store—the pioneer proprietor of the general mercantile being killed by eight Chinese for the gold in his safe.

Close to Jackson also are the sites of Hogtown, Suckertown and Helltown. And in Big Bar, another episode in the colorful career of Joaquin Murieta. An enterprising Frenchman in Big Bar offered the bandit a fine suit of chain armor for a thousand dollars. Murieta agreed it was a reasonable price if the steel was bullet proof. He forced the Frenchy to don the suit, fired several shots at it, point blank, and the only damage were a few blue and black marks. Murieta took the suit. It is not known why the bandit bothered to pay for it or where it was that fateful night when he met his death at Panoche Pass.

Not far from the tiny new camp of Drytown (which later would have twenty-six saloons) was a spring of good water where travelers between Sacramento and the southern mines would camp overnight. The water was used strictly for laundry and cooking purposes, judging by the accumu-lation of bottles around the spring, which caused the Mexican miners to call the spot Botilleas Spring.

A settlement grew up around the locality and the spring camp is now the site of the National Hotel in Jackson. The main part of town is largely made up of the old stone, iron-shuttered buildings but they are so altered as to be almost unrecognizable.

In 1850 the camp had grown considerably and demanded something better for a name than Botilleas Spring. Since Col. Alden Jackson had stopped at the original site longer than some and was credited with founding the town, his name was selected even though the gentleman had long since moved on to found Jacksonville, further south on the Tuolumne River.

By 1851 Jackson considered itself ready to become the county seat. It had almost eliminated the lawless element by stringing up ten men from the huge oak on Main Street and could see no reason for delaying the transfer from Double Springs. To expedite proceedings, the Jackson city fathers invited the dignitaries of Double Springs to a party at the largest local saloon. At the height of festivities, two Jackson men drove to the other town, loaded the county records, lock-stock-and-barrel, on a wagon and brought them back home. Next morning when the cold sober Double Springers found out what had happened it was too late to do anything about it.

Jackson was not able to hold the county seat honor very long however. At the regular election the next year it was found there had been a tremendous increase in the population of nearby Mokelumne Hill and the county seat was moved there—even after it was found the large vote had been accomplished by the industrious populace riding furiously from one polling place to another, casting votes like crazy. Mokelumne Hill held on for a decade then the county seat came back to Jackson.

As placer mining faded in smaller communities around Jackson, several deep quartz veins at the edge of the larger town began to yield a steady return. The Argonaut Mine was among the deepest in the world. Discovered in the '50s, it had a long period of discouragements but by the '70s it was established as a good producer. By 1930 it

HUGE TAILING WHEELS at Kennedy Mine, Jackson Gate near town of Jackson, are unique examples of efforts to dispose of silty refuse. Many mines and mills experienced difficulties removing waste—tailings—which tended to accumulate in stream to detriment of water supply and operations downstream.
Built in 1902, wheels are 68 feet high, raised tailings to vertical height of 48 feet. Each wheel was equipped with 176 buckets, belt drive and electric motor. Tops of elevators were connected to elaborate system of gravity flumes carrying liquid debris over top of nearby hill to dumps. Entire operation was once enclosed in sheet metal buildings. Kennedy Mine in background was one of giants of big hard rock days, reached depth of about a mile, making it one of the deepest gold mines in the U.S. according to California Division of Mines. At bottom of shafts are 150 miles of workings which produced gold, pyrites, quartz, galena, fluorapatite, sphalerite, ankerite, chalcopyrite and other carbonates. Mine has been idle since 1942.

had gone 6,300 feet into the earth and yielded well over $17 million.

A deep, narrow fissure in the rocks through which the creek flows gave the name Jackson Gate to the gulch a mile north of Jackson. Here were several rich mines, one of them operated by a woman and this one commanding a healthy re-spect from her masculine contemporaries. Not fully feminine to begin with, she affected pants and a man's red shirt, was known as Madame Pantaloon. Scorning any help from a mere man, except in a strictly business capacity, she accumulated a hundred thousand dollars from her claim and sold it for twenty more.

VOLCANO, CALIFORNIA

Ill-fated from the start, Volcano went through several periods of travail in its life as a gold camp which may well be characterized by its name. But since the name came before many of its troubles it is explained by the bare rocks resembling lava flow or by the crater-like valley which the town occupied. During the first feverish expansion of the original strike at Coloma, many of Col. Stevenson's regiment of New York Volunteers ranged the hills and valleys of the Sierra Piedmont and found rich deposits in this gulch formed like a volcano.

These first comers averaged $100 a day per pan, the better spots giving up $500. When snow began to fly that fall most of the men prudently retired to the lowlands since no one had taken valuable time to erect shelter. Yet two young soldier friends decided to disregard the ordinarily mild winter climate and stick it out. They left no record of the troubles they endured through the bitter cold but a band of Mexican prospectors found their bodies in the spring. The creek diggings were called Soldiers' Gulch.

That same spring Capt. John A. Sutter, trying to recoup his fortunes, attempted to mine the area with Long Toms manned by a retinue of Indians and South Sea Islanders. He did well for a while with low labor costs and little outlay for equipment but his system had outlasted its day. American miners on the scene raised an outcry that the captain was using "slave labor," not too far from the truth, and Sutter was forced to decamp or face a noose.

Volcano's troubles had begun. With the first soldier-prospectors, Mexicans, Americans and a goodly number of aborigines were working the gravels and there was only just so much space to work in. The Indians held no regard for the white man's claims, dipping their pans where they saw fit. Tension grew until a quarrelsome white claimed an Indian had stolen some of his equipment. The chief of the Indian camp said he would go to the tribesman's tent and search for the missing tool. When he turned his back, a trigger-happy Texas Ranger, Rod Stowell by name, let fly with his rifle. The killing of the chief precipitated the pint-sized "Volcano Indian War" which ended with several fatalities on both sides.

The next several years were no more peaceful but the camp grew rapidly and soon had a respectable group of buildings, one of the most elegant a Masonic Hall, among the first in California. It had a sumptuous bronze chandelier adorned with no less than twelve "coal oil" lamps. The whole assembly could be lowered to trim wicks and clean chimneys.

The native blue limestone was quarried and blocks dressed to provide excellent building material and this was used for the brewery, Lavezzo and Wells Fargo buildings, two-storied I.O.O.F. building, Adams Express office and wine shop. The handsome brick St. George Hotel with three floors is still in good condition. Unfortunately when the rotting balconies were repaired a few years ago the beautifully turned spindles were replaced by common boards. The little jail is a departure from the prevailing construction, made of sheet iron sandwiched between layers of two-inch lumber.

Volcano's nearest neighbor of consequence is Jackson, still a thriving town. In the '50s the two camps were of similar size with a natural rivalry between them, their respective newspapers not above making derogatory statements about each

FAMOUS "TWO SALOONS" BUILDING was duplex affair, double-barreled threat to sobriety, connected inside. Patrons sometimes became confused, thinking to make exit ran into another bar instead, had to have one more. One of the two saloons, The Jug, was last to close its doors, later acted as store and meeting place.

other. A Jackson visitor in Volcano attracted some attention when he plunked down a $20 gold piece to pay for his lodgings. The local miners gathered around to eye the coin and the Jackson man reported to his home papers that the Volcano populace was so backwoodsy it had never seen such a large piece of money before. The Volcano editor was incensed at this kind of slur and retaliated to the effect that it wasn't so much the novelty of the gold coin that caused so much amazement but the fact that the Jackson man had so much money in his possession and had actually paid his hotel bill instead of skipping town.

During the fabulous fifties Volcano began to show signs of maturity after its roistering days. A Thespian Society was organized and put on performances of such classics of the day as "The Iron Chest" and "She Stoops To Conquer" and wherever it could, often in the hall of the Fraternal Building at the head of the main street. During these first years the miners were starved for any kind of theatrical entertainment and it wasn't long before the amateur efforts were replaced by more practiced ones of traveling theatrical troupes from San Francisco, the actors going where the money was.

Not from the metropolis across the Bay but from Grass Valley came that darling of the miners, the child star Lotta Crabtree, to perform her Highland Fling and other dances under the watchful supervision of her mother, Mary Ann. This one night stand was very profitable, the miners throwing nuggets and coins on the stage in their enthusiasm for the black-eyed charmer, who was to go on from these pick-and-shovel towns to world tours on a career to net her millions.

A group of earnest Volcano citizens felt the miners needed more culture and gave them a lending library, one of the first in California, which lasted until all the books were borrowed and none returned. During the middle '50s a volunteer fire department staged hose drills and parades in the streets but was not too efficient at putting out fires which plagued the town.

Most flashy of the civic groups was a militia company called the "Volcano Blues." Its showpiece was a salute cannon which was merely an emblem until the Civil War broke out. Then the fire department, Volcano Blues and two other organizations banded together to form the Union Volunteers. When a minority group with Confederate sympathies threatened to divert the camp's gold supply to Southern uses, the cannon christ-

LITTLE ASSAY OFFICE was operated by Madera Brothers through busy years of town—except for first few when mining was all by pan, Long Tom or rocker, and gold was self-evident. Later prospectors from hills with ore samples needed assayer's valuation. After Volcano died as mining camp, structure was taken over by Jack Giannini for barber shop. Another Giannini from Volcano founded Bank of America and Angelo Rossi, former mayor of San Francisco was born in Volcano.

ened "Old Abe," was wheeled out into the open. It might have been more of a threat if some Union man had thought to provide cannon balls. Instead some round cobblestones were fired with indifferent success but enough noise to discourage the Rebel cause in Volcano and the great Civil War engagement came to an end.

AMADOR CITY, CALIFORNIA

A small group of Argonauts detached itself from the hordes swarming over the Sierra foothills and started panning the sands of Amador Creek in 1848. The tiny band had great faith in the chosen location even though little gold turned up in their pans to justify it.

Pickings grew ever smaller until the claim was exhausted and the men ready to fold their tents and fade away. Then in 1851 came the big strike. The original miners had been trying to get their gold the easy way, out of the creek gravels, but the bonanza was found in the quartz vein of the Mother Lode itself at the point where it intersected with Amador Creek.

The find was not made by an experienced miner but by a Baptist preacher, a Reverend Davidson. Not being able to do the hard work or handle the finances he took in other members of the cloth as partners. The popular name for the workings was naturally—"The Ministers' Claim." The mine was later consolidated with six other workings, the combine called the "Original Amador," a complex of more than nine miles of crosscuts, drifts and raises. They opened up from a 1,238 foot inclined shaft. Total production was almost $4 million.

Better known and far more productive was the Keystone Mine. It was first dug in '53 and for several early years the ore was crushed in the primitive quartz mills called by the Mexican name of arrastres. Later more modern stamp mills were built and as their capacities increased the underground workings developed a shaft 2,680 feet deep. A large portion of the ore was of an unusual sulfarsenide type but it yielded $25 million.

Amador City is two and a half miles northwest of Sutter Creek and is similiar to it in history and general background. Sutter Creek was named for the man who had once operated the vast agricultural domain of Sutter's Fort where Sacramento stands today. Sutter had set up the sawmill at Coloma to supply lumber for his buildings. Instead, gold was discovered in the millrace and the subsequent rush of gold seekers destroyed Sutter's dream by depleting his help and overrunning his farms. He made a pitiful attempt to follow the "If you can't lick 'em, join 'em" school but failed utterly, principally because he had no aptitude for handling his help along the lines the American miners demanded. They claimed his system was "slave labor" and Sutter was forced to quit his claims at Sutter Creek.

More spectacular was the career of Leland Stanford in the same area. Having made a little money in Sacramento as a merchant he bought into the Lincoln Mine. At first there was nothing but trouble and at one time he was ready to sell out for $5,000. His foreman, Robert Dowes, persuaded him to hang on, the strike at last was made and Stanford was established as a tycoon. With his partners he then built his railroad, became U. S. Senator, then Governor of California and founded Stanford University.

OLD IMPERIAL — finest hotel in Amador City. Bar section operated until fairly recent years, barkeep in fancy vest pouring drinks for fewer and fewer patrons until forced to quit.

FIDDLETOWN, CALIFORNIA

The year of first discoveries of gold in the Sierra foothills was drawing to a close when a party of prospectors found rich deposits in the gravel of a creek entering the Consumnes River. So absorbed were they in sloshing out a few dollars to the pan no one noticed darkening skies until the first downpour of the winter season forced them to seek cover. Only then did they think of building makeshift shelter.

The winter was a wet one, continued rains forcing the men from Missouri who made up the bulk of the settlers to stay in their flimsy houses. Most of them had played the fiddle for dances "back home" and they now spent most of their time scraping out "Turkey In The Straw" and other nostalgic melodies. It was "moughty blamed natural" to name the town—Fiddletown.

This was as wild a camp as any in the Mother Lode. Eighty-two-year-old Thomas Davis who lived in Fiddletown many years is quoted by the San Francisco Examiner as saying: "There was plenty of activity and violence. I always remember mother's description of a Saturday night when the miners had come to town after a horse race. One man was leaning against the pillar of the hotel porch when an enemy knifed him. He clutched the pillar, spinning around several times before he hit the ground, dead." Another incident is related by N. B. Randall who runs the museum housed in Schallhorn's Wagon Shop: "The storekeeper shipped millions in gold out of town. He knew robbers were after him and barricaded his store. But one afternoon when he came back from a trip he found the men inside it. They killed him with a hatchet."

While all this was going on many other camps were springing up in the area fringing on the Consumnes, most of them with names reflecting the circumstances of their founding—French Flat, Drytown, Loafer Flat, Suckertown, American Hill, Arkansas Hill, Yankee Hill, Plymouth.

Fiddletown itself flourished. Although the placers petered out, hydraulic mining came in and paid huge dividends. Buildings were going up all along the main street, much more substantial than the jerry-built structures of the first winter. A deposit of rhyolite tuff had been discovered close by, and since this material is easily worked when first uncovered, hardening on exposure, it was used extensively. Other buildings used bricks made of clay found nearby and fired in a local kiln. Others went up with schist blocks accurately

RAMMED EARTH ADOBE OFFICE of Dr. Yee near center of Fiddletown's Chinatown. Genial Oriental escaped ostracism suffered by most of race in gold rush days, his sunny smile and expert dispensing of herbs winning hearts of miners. Original roof of shingles was replaced by sheet metal which served in its mundane way to protect venerable structure from usual fate of adobes, melting away when roof deteriorated. Present tenant, Yow Fong Chow, is sole remaining representative of 2,000 Chinese once living in Fiddletown, popularly known as Jimmy. Note original iron shutters at windows, typical of period but not always used on adobe buildings.

cut and fitted. And elegant marble, quarried locally, was given such utilitarian use as lining the basement of Henry Schroeder's Brewery.

Allen A. Woolfolk, old timer in the place, tells of some early structures, most of them now gone. There was a dance hall built by a Mr. Eaurow, two blacksmith shops—Pigeon's and McClary's. Four hotels took care of the transient and some of the permanent residents—the N. S., St. Charles, Flag and the ostentatious Charlesville. Charles Hikinson ran a large livery stable which was destroyed by fire as were most of the frame buildings in this and other towns. The Farnham's lumber yard and their lumber-built home were spared those holocausts and the house stands today. It is owned by George Pacini, an Italian grape grower. This fruit has figured in the history of the town from the beginning of the hydraulic period. The winery in those days was run by Peter Smith and Sons who had their own vineyard. Fiddletown's Chi-

nese population was as high as 2,000 with the usual assortment of stores, medicine shops, joss houses and opium dens.

Two judges held jurisdiction over the community, as colorful as any magistrates in the gold rush country. On one occasion, it is related, Judge Yates listened to a long-drawn-out case in which one of the witnesses was displaying a complete and obvious disregard of the truth. His patience at last giving way, he brought his gavel down hard and thundered: "This court is adjourned!" He allowed the contrasting silence for a moment and then blasted: "This man is a damn liar!" After another pause he lowered his voice dramatically. "I declare this court in session."

The other jurist, Judge Purinton, made frequent trips to San Francisco and Sacramento and became increasingly annoyed at the titters when he wrote "Fiddletown" after his name on hotel registers. When his indignation reached its limit, he pulled some legal strings and had the town's name changed to the more dignified one of Oleta.

The town accepted this gesture to propriety for a few years then the more fitting Fiddletown was restored. The place now drowses in a pleasant bower of grape vineyards, prune and walnut orchards, green pastures where stock grazes. The old wild days are long gone and the camp is bypassed by most tourists. Some of the few remaining residents would like to see more of them stop, the rest wish to retain the peace and quiet which now hangs over Fiddletown like a golden haze on a summer day.

HOME OF MRS. L. E. FRINCHABOY who s u p p l i e d photographer with much of Fiddletown facts. Beautiful example of frame architecture of the period house was finished 100 years ago, built by young Mr. Chestnut as a home for his intended bride, Patience Neff. Couple moved in later that year. Mrs. Frinchaboy, her husband and three sons (who served in both World Wars) moved into house in 1939. House contains many interesting relics such as fireplace of local marble. Famed violinist David Rubinoff, long honorary "Mayor" of Fiddletown, frequently visits old camp with family, staying overnight as guests of Mrs. Frinchaboy.

SCHALLHORN BLACKSMITH AND WAGON SHOP was erected in 1870 of rectangular blocks, 12x18x20, of Valley Springs rhyolite tuff. Source of material is one and a half miles out of town. Builder Chris Schallhorn sawed most of blocks himself, built sturdy wagons in shop for many years. Building now serves as part-time museum, proprietor Randall "closing shop" when mood dictates.

EL DORADO and SHINGLE SPRINGS, CALIFORNIA

Mud Springs—a name to conjure with but not to mention to your mother. Yet that was the camp's name. The first seekers of gold there gathered around the water supply in such numbers they trampled the ground into a quagmire—and the camp had a name—Mud Springs.

In addition to attracting an increasing number of Argonauts, Mud Springs was an important stop on the old Carson Emigrant Trail and it soon became a crossroads station for freight and stage lines. At the height of the gold rush the population mounted to several thousands, the town complete with "full quota of saloons, hotels, and a gold production that gave its citizens just cause for pride." It was during this period the town was incorporated and this same civic pride caused a change in the name to El Dorado.

Picturesque place names are also in evidence at some of the neighboring camps which sprang up during the gold rush and have since disappeared —Loafer's Hollow, Deadman's Hollow, Dry Creek, Missouri Flat, Empire Ravine and Shingle Springs.

Though rich while they lasted, the original placer deposits were quickly exhausted. Then the lode mines came into being and for a time there was a continuous line of quartz mills extending south to the crossing on the Consumnes River, the spot then called Saratoga and later Huse Bridge. The stamp mills were of varying capacities, the one at Logtown, a mile or two from El Dorado, having eight stamps.

A good many of the more important buildings were erected on ground later found to be rich in gold and the miners waited impatiently for them to be considered outmoded or "menaces to health and safety," so they could wreck them and mine the sites. Ten thousand dollars in gold was said to have been extracted from the soil where the dance hall stood.

El Dorado's near neighbor, Shingle Springs, gained its cognomen from its shingle mill and a fine spring of very cold water. The Shingle Spring House was built in 1850 of lumber brought around the Horn and had an apparent knack of spawning brawls in the lustier days.

Mining there began that same year, the surrounding gulches filled with cabins, most of them hastily thrown together. For the first few years the miners were forced to get their supplies from Buckeye Flat (named by men homesick for their native Ohio) but by '57 a store was established at the camp. This was a commentary on the slow development of Shingle Springs and of its rather small gold deposits. Most of the gold camps grew so rapidly stores and supply houses sprang up within a few days or weeks of the first strikes.

Prosperity did suddenly smile on Shingle Springs but from an entirely different direction. In '65 the Sacramento Valley Railroad extended its line from the camp to Latrobe. For two years Shingle Springs enjoyed a top place in the ranks of gold towns and then fell flat. The Central Pacific Railroad from Sacramento via Auburn diverted the overland traffic from the Placerville Road and Shingle Springs reverted to the status of a village.

WELLS FARGO BUILDING — most impressive and unaltered remnant in El Dorado — Shingles Springs district. Also housed Phelps Store. Constructed of semi-dressed native stone, it is impressive with deep-set, arched doors in upper and lower stories. Structure once boasted elaborate balcony. Peaked roof, common in gold country, is intact where disappeared from most other buildings. Even brick chimney remains sound.

"**Wild flowers had grown there . . . and even they were dead!**"

LEESBURG, IDAHO

"We heard a whooping and a shouting and looking up the hill we saw Mulkey waving his hat and hollering like the Indians were after him. We scrambled up the steep, rocky bank to see what the matter was. A big tree had blown over in the previous winter's storms and the roots had dragged up a lot of quartz with them. The stuff was loaded with gold, so rich we were all very much excited and breakfast got all burned up."

So reads the diary of Frank Barney Sharkey, one of a party of six prospectors, banded together for greater safety against hostile Indians. In July of 1866 they reached the banks of the Salmon River, Idaho's "River Of No Return," Lige Mulkey being delegated to cook breakfast that morning and do the camp chores. After he had the food on the fire he set off up the hill after the horses and made the rich find. Once reprovisioned, the men could never find that particular spot again but they did discover one of the richest placering grounds in all mining history, those of the Leesburg basin.

Frank Sharkey was born in Eastport, Maine January 8, 1838. At 14 he stowed away with another boy on the square-rigged brig Black Duck. "We had a hard time of it," he wrote, "having nothing to eat but hardtack but managed to steal some salt pork to go with it. We were 63 days on this trip, saw Cardiff, Wales, and Liverpool before coming back."

Hearing wonderful tales of the gold fields in California he decided to go there. "In the winter of 1854-55, I sailed from New York around Cape Horn and landed in San Francisco, getting my first job in Oroville, delivering meat by wagon around town. It was a team of Spanish horses, wild and hard to manage. I had not worked very long when they ran away with me and smashed the wagon and harness all up." His next job was at the Cape Claim, a mile above town, where he tended the pine knots burning in the dark tunnels so miners could see to work. He got good wages for a job, $3.50 a day, and got acquainted with another youth doing the same work. When the pair grew tired of working regularly, they pooled their knowledge of mining and decided to go into business for themselves.

They went to Compton on the upper Yuba River, invested their small savings and promptly lost them. Their next project in the spring brought them only expenses but they stayed with it two years. Young Sharkey had been getting more and more homesick but after he sailed to Maine, stayed only a few months and took ship again for California, this time by the Isthmus of Panama. He served for a time in the California Volunteers and after being discharged, went to Portland, Oregon, where he spent the winter of 1861-62.

Frank Sharkey had by this time established a pattern of wanderlust that was to prevail the rest

OLD LOG BUILDINGS OF LEESBURG sag toward collapse, one at left serving as post office during years of activity in fabulous gold camp. Until discovery of gold in Leesburg Basin by Sharkey and party, beaver pelts had been medium of exchange. Buffalo, black-tailed deer and elk in Basin were killed for food and hides, mountain sheep retreating to higher elevations. Now with solitude prevailing, they venture into grassy meadows between log houses.

of his life. Working in one camp after another, he "fell in with" Lige Mulkey and William Smith. Outfitting early in the spring of 1863 the trio went up to French Gulch in the upper Columbia country, prospected all summer and gradually drifted toward the Montana diggings. They expected to get over the Coeur d'Alene Mountains before winter set in but on arriving at the old mission at Cataldo, they found themselves snowed in and turned back to spend the winter on the Spokane prairie.

Early the next spring, before the grass had start-

ed, they tried again, making a break to get out by following around Lake Pend Oreille, keeping their horses alive with rushes from the lake, cottonwood bark and young aspen buds. There was a constant plague of Indians but they made their way to Jocko, Montana, where the Indian agent, Angus McDonald, fed them. After resting a few days they pushed on to Bannack, then to Alder Gulch and Virginia City. They worked in various camps until the fall of 1865. "That was the fall they were hanging so many road agents, especially at Bannack," Sharkey recorded.

IMMENSE PILES OF BOULDERS line Napias Creek for miles, residue of dredge which worked stream of gold during years following crude hand methods. Additional millions in yellow metal were salvaged by mechanical monster which worked in a pond of its own making, then moved to another, scooping up mouthfuls of rocks and gravel digesting it for gold, spewing out barren waste behind.

Next summer the adventurers arrived in what would later be known as the Leesburg Basin. There more hardy pioneers joined them—Ward Girton, Joseph Rapp and one Hendricks. "Hendricks," said Barney Sharkey, "Proved to be a very disagreeable partner so we got rid of him at French Gulch." The group had now hardened into the five which constituted the Discovery Party.

As they were coming down the North Fork of the Salmon River, Sharkey noted: "We were surprised to see a man almost naked out in the river. He was jumping around in the water grabbing at something and we found out later he was trying to catch salmon. His name was Mose Miller and he had been prospecting in the central Idaho country. Learning of Quantrell, he had started out to join him but ran out of provisions and clothes. Almost all he had left was a good mule."

The five went on to Napias Creek, named by the Indians for their word meaning "money", because they had found gold nuggets in the gravels which they would exchange for food and trinkets. The prospectors followed up Napias Creek, panning all the way, and thoroughly, since no gold has been found along their route.

While some of the men were pitching camp one night in July, 1866, Sharkey and Bill Smith sank the usual prospect hole. As soon as they struck bedrock a pan of the bottom gravel was sloshed out. There in the bottom were many of the sought after yellow flakes, about a dollar and a quarter's worth. The next panful yielded even more and the men attending to the chores heard the jubilant shouts—"We've struck the biggest diggings ever struck!" All evening routine work was abandoned. Supper had to wait until it was too dark to pan, the meal prepared by the light of the camp fire and hardly tasted.

The spot of the first big find was just above the mouth of Ward's Gulch. Being thorough, even though excited, the men prospected the immediate neighborhood so as to properly file their claims before the news leaked out. Every hole they sank on Napias Creek, in Ward's Gulch, Bear Track and Discovery Bar showed wonderful prospects. Subsequent mining operations proved the claims, several miles apart, had been sunk in the richest ore.

Plans were made to keep the find secret until the men could let their friends in on the good thing, the finders being entitled to only two claims, one by right of discovery, one by right of location. In order to file the claims and lay in a store of supplies, it was necessary to go the Montana diggings, the nearest settled area. Almost immediately Lige Mulkey became very sick and Frank Sharkey was delegated to look after him while the others went on. Mulkey got worse, lapsing into a delirium, calling for his mother. "Here I am, son," Sharkey volunteered. Mulkey turned over, gave him a hard look and asked: "Who are you?" Sharkey said: "I'm your mother," to which the sick man replied with scorn—"Well, you're a hell of a looking mother!"

A party of Indians arrived at the camp next day and asked Sharkey if he had found any napias. When the reply was "No," the spokesman retorted "Ishump!" which meant "you lie!" It appeared the Indians had panned out some of the dirt in the prospect holes and found rich gold and now they said this country was no good for thieving white men and they had better get out or else. Sharkey pointed to the sick man and promised they would leave as soon as he could travel. The braves were appeased to some extent and as soon as Mulkey could walk with Sharkey's help, the pair started off.

The rest of the party had made good time toward the Montana diggings but as they were going up the Lemhi, they were surprised to meet a group heading for "the new diggings at Leesburg," the news having traveled on ahead. The party outfitted, reprovisioned and returned to their camp to find a roaring body of several hundred miners.

Sharkey and Mulkey rejoined their partners there and by August 10, 1866, there were several thousand at the new camp of Leesburg. The diary reads: "We worked our claims for several years and took out a lot of gold dust. The average clean up for the first three years was a pan two-thirds full of dust. We hired a bunch of men to work for us and paid them at the average rate of $7 a day. Our discovery party took out the most money during the first two years."

With friendly interest a stranger watched Sharkey at his work one day. The miner scooped up some dirt on his shovel and panned out over a dollar's worth of gold. The stranger let out an excited cry but not over the gold, he explained. His name was Fred Phillips and he had a large stock of merchandise in Helena. He knew now he had found a good place to set up a store. He rounded up his partner, David McNutt, the two of them retrieving the Helena stock to set up the first store in Leesburg.

John H. Wheeler brought in the supplies each fall from then on, but from Salt Lake City. Everything had to come by mule train so a year's stock of food and other needs was packed in each trip. A unique "delivery service" was set up at the central merchandise store in Leesburg. The concern maintained a large bunch of burros in a nearby corral and a miner would cinch his purchases on the back of one and drive it home. After unloading, the burro was turned loose to return promptly to the store.

Leesburg's population was of the roughest sort, most of the men soldiers fresh from the Civil War, and feelings still ran very high between them. Southern sympathizers were in the majority and they had been successful in getting the camp named for General Lee. There was a big celebration with an ample flow of liquor at the "christening," the Northerners conspicuous by their absence. They had removed all their belongings, lock-stock and barrel, to a new site some distance up the gulch and named their town Grantsville. But before long tempers cooled and back came the Northern rebels.

The town boomed to a population of about seven thousand in a few years while operating placers in the stream bed. Some estimates of the amount of gold removed go as high as $40 million, much of this in "coarse gold," some in nuggets. After the wasteful white miners saw the gold was playing out, at least for their hand methods, they allowed an eager Chinese band to move in and start more patient extraction, themselves extracting a stiff fee for the privilege. The section where the Orientals settled became a hot bed of vice, sanctuary for opium smokers and line of crib houses filled with girls imported from the poorest peasant areas of China. In 1879 the Chinese population was massacred and robbed. The one individual remaining maintained the act was done by white men and not the "Sheepeater" Indians who were publicly blamed.

About the time the gravels seemed thoroughly exhausted, a dredge was built on the spot from parts hauled up the steep canyons. This monster chewed up the whole valley, leaving behind it piles of digested rock excrement to make the most enduring monuments to the fast decaying Leesburg.

By 1946 the last two remaining residents of the town had moved down to more comfortable Salmon City, the post office was closed and telephone line taken down. Only Leesburg's ghosts knew the dead streets.

CATALDO MISSION built in 1848 with use of Indian labor. Wooden pegs take place of nails, mud from river spread over walls for plaster. Two paintings beside altar represent Heaven and Hell, were done with Indian vegetable dyes. It was here Frank Barney Sharkey rested in fall of 1863 on prospecting trip to Montana diggings, journey was eventually leading to immense wealth at Leesburg. At mission men were told heavy snows would prevent their crossing mountains until spring. After pause here they returned to "Spokane Prairie" for winter.

REMAINS OF LEESBURG consist of two lines of log structures on only street left. Some have had shingles or shake roofs replaced by tin during first World War years and are in fair condition. Others are in state of decay, one with stream running through it. Only semblance of two-story building remaining is seen in foreground. Early day ad in Leesburg newspaper states: "Several substantial log houses furnished with ample supply of wood are available for immediate occupancy at a rental rate of $5 per day."

BAY HORSE, IDAHO

If Leesburg had been able to satisfy all who came looking for riches, Bay Horse might well have been a horse of a different color or not in the running at all. As it was, Leesburg had a disappointed overflow in the early 1870s, a few of whom went sifting the bottoms of Bay Horse Creek flowing into the Salmon River, the "River Of No Return", and they found a little gold.

Hopes for another booming gold camp faded out quickly with the realization that the gold was fading too, and Bay Horse was almost a ghost before it had a body to emerge from. But there in some heavy iron ore deposits was a rich vein of silver, life and hopes springing up anew. Not so glamorous as gold but solid wealth just the same.

How to get capital to get the silver out of the rock, to build mills and smelters? It was going to be a hard job. There were no roads in the area, all hauling of machinery and supplies would have to be done by mule train. But in '79 a toll road

was started, coming from Challis and reaching to Bonanza. It was completed in '81, with a spur to Salmon due to the prosperity of Leesburg, and the way was open for big-scale silver mining at Bay Horse.

The first extraction was readily achieved, the white metal being largely "free," pure veins of it running through the ore, a quantity of valuable lead saved the same time. However, to the grief of miners and investors, the silver was more finely divided as the vein grew deeper, the iron ore containing it more refractory—the Bay Horse's easy wealth was little more than a dream.

Its best years were in the '80s and '90s but the mines continued to operate in a desultory fashion until 1915 when the whole town shut down and almost everybody moved away. In 1920 there was a brief revival when a optimistic mining concern thought it had the answer to hard-to-get silver. Rising costs and stable income from silver soon defeated this effort and Bay Horse

ROW OF CHARCOAL OVENS once had seven units, five now more or less intact. Beehive-like structures were used to make charcoal for fuel in large smelter which extracted pure silver and lead from ores mined at Bay Horse. Surrounding hills, once covered with virgin timber were denuded for wood to supply ovens, are now sparsely covered again with second growth trees. Stray cattle use ovens for shelter in severe winter storms and for shade on hot days.

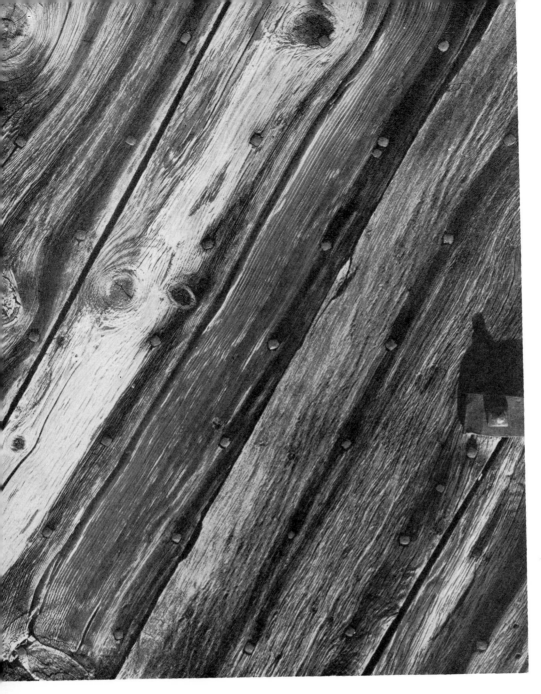

DOOR OF STORAGE HOUSE for blasting powder s h o w s weathering of s e v e n t y years, square heads of hand-forged nails and bolts.

was scratched again, this time to stay out. One man lives there now, making visitors welcome after venturing up the steep road but is "scared to death" when some of them climb over the ruins or scale the coke ovens all of which are ready to crumble at any moment.

There is a tiny cemetery just below the Bay Horse remains. Twenty years ago there were still a few headboards standing there. Those bearing distinguishable markings spelled out sad tales of soldiers killed in battle with Indians. It is a one-sided story, there being no record there of the banishing of the natives from their hunting grounds, their homes and burial places. The markers showing where their attackers died have

gone to dust, and fading are the memories of the original inhabitants.

Most of the vanished dates on those headboards were in the 1860s, the period of the Indian trouble. Another cemetery just above the town and somewhat better preserved, contains some legible markers. These show dates beginning in the early '80s when the mining town was getting started and the first fatalities took place. Natural deaths were few, most resulting from accidents in the mines and violence. The miners spent few evenings pursuing culture, doing their relaxing in the several drinking emporiums on both sides of the one steeply-sloping street. Arguments often started spontaneously and ended with gunfire.

Sometimes these affairs had the comic side. One tale concerns a quarrel between Bill Smith, one of the founders of Leesburg, and a Jim Hayden which took place at a nearby camp. The men had been drinking for some hours when hostilities broke out over some trifle. Flaming mad, Smith drew his gun, a "short-barreled pocket pistol," and fired several shots at Hayden. The aim was good but the victim did not crumple. It seems Hayden was wearing a pair of common-type pants made of heavy wool and thickly "foxed" with several layers of buckskin.

PRESENT DAY SCENE ON MAIN STREET of Bay Horse is peaceful, contrasting with boisterous days when silver mining was big industry. Saloons and boarding houses for single miners and smelter workers filled gaps between existing buildings. Tall, false-front structure had pool hall and saloon on ground floor, rooms for rent upstairs. Another saloon and store stood next, then stone shell standing. It was used for many purposes at different times including newspaper office and post office. Although appearing solid in front, it is in state of collapse in rear. Further on were more business houses and across from these at right stood a large pretentious structure described as a "girlie house."

SHOUP, IDAHO

In 1881 the Salmon River was so full of those noble beauties "you could almost walk across on their backs." It was a fact mule teams often balked at fording it, finding the swarms of salmon disconcerting to their careful steps in the swift current. Bears, it seemed, liked the situation.

It is not written that Sam James and Pat O'Hara were impressed with the salmon. They had gold on their minds having found the claims around Leesburg quite thoroughly worked out. Their spirits were as low as the canyon walls of the Salmon were high when they camped on one of its banks where Pine Creek tumbled in. The next morning they panned more color than they had anywhere along the stream.

They worked hard and got increasingly large amounts of gold and then very little. Leaving the creek they went up the cliff which overlooked the spot where the gravels had been richest—and sure enough, here was the vein that had yielded the placer grains.

That first hard rock discovery became the Grunter Mine. In rapid succession were developed the Lost Miner, Hummingbird, True Fissure and Spring Lode. Partner James tired of the responsibilities of running a large mine and sold out his share for $5,000. By 1890 more than three hundred claims had been filed in the area, not all of them delivering profit.

As soon as the camp showed signs of permanence, the miners tried to agree on a name for it. The town had developed on the only semi-level spot, the banks of the Salmon, thickly studded with huge rocks. A popular vote decided on "Boulder" and the choice was sent to Washington. Authority rejected the name in favor of "Shoup," as an honor to Governor Shoup who had been extremely prominent in all early Salmon River country affairs.

As in other early day mining camps one of the hardest problems to solve was getting supplies in. The main sources were established camps, Virginia City and Bannack in Montana, Salt Lake City in Utah. When trails became passable in the spring, traders hurried in with loaded pack animals. As soon as the population warranted it, these single mules and burros were augmented by organized strings of assorted beasts of burden, mules favored as being more sure-footed on steep mountain trails and for their load carrying capacity.

Prices for goods brought in fluctuated widely in supply and demand ratio and on the care that had to be taken to deliver the supplies in good condition. The Salmon City *Recorder-Herald* listed sugar at 80¢ a pound, butter $1, tea $3.50, salt $1, soap $1 a bar, yeast powder $1 for a small can, tomatoes $1.50 a can, oysters $1, lard 85¢ and beef 20¢ a pound, coal oil $8 a gallon and tobacco $3 a pound.

Shoup has been dead as a mining town for many years. A fishing resort occupies the site now and interest for the ghost town hunters centers in the area just past the town where there are many remains of the old mills and mines.

MOUTH OF MINE TUNNEL shoots out draft of air at 42 degrees, startling on hot summer day. Little wooden wagon was not usual ore conveyance, iron ore cars more common. Door was kept padlocked to discourage thieves, temptation being strong in heyday of Shoup mining when "blossom rocks"—ore heavily laced with gold—was common. Shovel seems to be ready for use although had stood idle many years.

"The flame guttered . . . then seemed to be pinched out!"

CURLEW, WASHINGTON

Always a bridesmaid, never a bride—that was the story of Curlew. It was named for a water bird and a lake where they abounded but it never had a name for gold.

Curlew had its beginings in a very modest way in the '80s with a few trappers' cabins. Since the soil was rich and comparatively free of trees and stumps, a few farmers built homes and fenced some fields. A school and a few stores were built.

During the early years life in Curlew was peaceful. Occasionally some prospector would come into town claiming he had struck gold in the hills and there was a flurry of excitement. The news was readily accepted each time since the wish was there and lots of gold had been found in Republic and other nearby camps. But alas, nothing ever materialized from these claims except grubstakes by the gullible storekeepers.

Curlew had settled back into a succession of naps when the actual bombshell exploded. "The railroad is coming!" The Spokane and British Columbia announced plans for a line through Republic, Kettle Falls, Curlew and Grand Forks in Canada. The Great Northern already had an option on the only logical right-of-way but that did not deter the S. & B. C. from making a great show of surveying another one alongside. An elaborate station was built on the hill above Curlew—then the long, empty pause. The investors

J. C. KIEHL who has lived in Curlew since before the days when the "Hot Air Railroad" made numerous false starts toward construction which never materialized. He stands here at side door of Ansorge Hotel where he now resides. Small false-front stood here first, erected by Ansorge and used as restaurant. To make room for hotel it was moved around to side, facetiously referred to as "Ansorge Annex."

COPY OF OLD PICTURE loaned by J. C. Kiehl shows Ansorge Hotel in days of first World War. Jitney service operated by Kiehl was in full swing, taxis shown here lined up and ready to go. Several loungers on porch seem not too interested in proceedings.

ANSORGE HOTEL at right, now more than commodious home for Mr. and Mrs. J. C. Kiehl, two of Curlew's oldest inhabitants. Mr. Kiehl remembers: "There were many times in the old days when the hotel was so full they had to put extra cots in the hallways. Those were the war days and I ran a jitney service for drummers and prospectors. It seems like they wanted to go everywhere, around town and out to the neighboring towns, even to Republic. Those boys were always good pay and sometimes gave me tips." Building at left was old Maxwell Meat Market.

MANY BOARDED UP FALSE-FRONTED STORES line streets of one-time flourishing Curlew. Most breaks in ranks caused by fires which took heavy toll in days when frame structures were tinder dry, water pressure low.

were wondering where their money had gone when more surveys were ordered and the "notch on the hill" was deepened to a more respectable cut. Now, everybody thought, we are really on our way to having a railroad through town. Real estate values advanced and property changed hands.

Again the interminable wait. The grumbling of citizens grew louder. "That new railroad is nothing but a lot of hot air!" was shouted and the Spokane and British Columbia was always called "The Hot Air Railroad" through the years, the line never being completed. Eventually the Great Northern exercised its option and Curlew 'did have trains, but it was too late. All hopes of a big gold discovery had long since vanished and Curlew was just a whistle stop.

ST. PATRICK'S CATHOLIC CHURCH built in 1903 and kept in good repair now has scant congregation. Barren hills surrounding town once had good growth of timber, were stripped to provide wood and lumber.

REPUBLIC, WASHINGTON

John Welty was discouraged after a whole summer of prospecting along the streams in northeastern Washington. When winter snows covered the ground he got a job for the winter, glad of a respite from clawing over the rugged mountains. But wanderlust and the ever-present hope of a good strike pulled him out along the streams at the very first break in the weather. In the middle of February, 1896, he did make that strike, and in the same stream he had worked the fall before —Granite Creek.

The resultant boom was such that by the first of May that year, Republic had a name and newspaper—the *Republic Pioneer*. On the 14th of the month it reported with a glow: "Here is a little city that is moving right along. Large quantities of whiskey, flour and other necessities arrived during the week."

By fall the camp had fifty log and canvas shacks, five stores, three blacksmith shops, four restaurants, two hotels, two fruit and cigar stores, two meat markets, three livery stables, three bakeries, three assay offices, tailor, shoemaker, doctor, jeweler and the usual lot of saloons. The Miners' Union sponsored big dances held in Patsy Clark's big boarding house. No cemetery existed until a young woman was found strangled "by persons unknown" and her body was the means to a permanent burial place on the steep hillside. The first school was a tent in the brush of the creek bottom, soon replaced by a log building. Indians were welcomed in the school and at first outnumbered the white pupils.

By 1900 a large part of Republic's growth was in the direction of brothels and saloons, the latter numbering up to twenty-eight, with six dance halls going strong, night and day. As late as 1940 an elaborate Opera House remained from those days. It was described as having an "elegant false front, copiously ornamented with balconies, each of which had a railing supported by fancy turned spindles." Republic now serves the surrounding farmers and vacationers, the days long vanished when the roistering miners found many easy ways to spend their money.

ORIGINAL ALTAR is intact in old Church of the Immaculate Conception in Republic, Wash. Edifice stands on steep hillside, conspicuous for miles around.

ORIENT, WASHINGTON

Gold had been discovered on the shoulder of First Thought Mountain and there was a certainty something big would come of it. Alec Ireland platted the town of Orient in 1900 and Mr. and Mrs. George Temple drove a wagon there from Bossburg which was then a thriving place, establishing a homestead the following year.

Gold hopes were slow being realized. There were no loose placer grains in the stream and it took time to interest big money for hard rock mining. Ireland, Billy Stiles and the Temples were at first the only residents of Orient, the latter proving up their claim and in 1904 receiving their ownership papers signed by President Theodore Roosevelt. They worked hard on the farm and Temple started a stage line from Bossburg to Republic, and up to Greenwood and Phoenix—a big mining camp in Canada—and Grand Forks, also across the border.

As the mines developed in a big way, Temple got much business hauling machinery, particularly for the Easter Sunday and Little Gem Mines. There were several other prosperous operations, one named after the mountain looming over the town—First Thought. This mine was also the main course of the economic development of Orient although its name came from another mine, the Orient.

Two quartz mills were set up, one at the First Thought, the other at the Gold Stake. By this time Orient had grown into a bustling town. "It was a very lively place," says Mrs. Leslie Gourlie, daughter of the Temples, "We had five saloons, two big livery stables, several stores and three hotels. These were whipsaw-shacky places, called by their owners names — Mrs. Reynolds, Mrs. Hayes and Mrs. Arnold. All three were pretty good cooks, doing the best they could under the circumstances. The best food, however, was available to the men at the mine cook houses. Most of the single ones ate there, slept in the bunk houses and lived quiet lives during the week. But on Saturday nights they'd come down to town and cut loose. What wild times they had, spending most of their money just that one night. There were plenty of loose women and lots of hard liquor to help them do it, too."

When the Great Northern Railroad made plans to run its line to Republic, George Temple ceded the right of way through his land, as he did later for the highway. During the hectic days of railroad construction there was a boom, the hotels full and Mrs. Temple feeding many of the men in the tiny homestead cabin.

When asked if Orient is permanently finished, Mrs. Gourlie replied: "Oh, no. There is lots of gold in the mines yet. They have barely scratched the surface. Most are down only about a hundred and fifty feet, none more than three hundred. All we need is an advance in the price of gold. Of course the machinery is getting all rusty and likely will be badly out of date. But the people who are still living here are hopeful that something good will happen to the town. We really haven't had any activity since the first World War."

ORIENT FIRE DEPARTMENT did its best when fire broke out in Orient but best was often not enough. Many buildings burned because of tinder dry condition and insufficient water pressure. Fancy tower in background is crowning glory of school which once held several hundred pupils. Structure was fixed up several years ago and is in good repair but now serves only handful of children.

NORTHPORT, WASHINGTON

A few miles below the United States-Canada line the Columbia River flows past the sleepy old town of Northport, once one of the most roistering mining camps in the state of Washington. At this point below Silver Crown Mountain the Columbia is wider than it used to be, now forming Roosevelt Lake by waters backed up from Grand Coulee Dam.

In April of 1892 the only means of travel here was along a mountain trail and at the future site of Northport there were only three homesteaders' cabins. Yet a few short months later the place had a newspaper, the *Northport News,* its little press hauled in by ox team and set up in the huddle of tents and shacks. The first issue came out on July 4th, greeting the community: "It is already a town. Tomorrow—a few tomorrows hence, at any rate—it will be a city."

A forest fire threatened the dry buildings that first summer, only a change in wind saving them. In September the railroad reached town and Northport was on its way to become "the future mining, milling, smelting and agricultural city of north-

eastern Washington. There followed a series of disastrous fires and after each the town was rebuilt, each time more permanently so that today the buildings remaining are of brick. One striking exception is the huge frame brothel.

After fire came flood. With the spring freshets of 1894 the Columbia rose far above normal. All of Northport down along the flat was swept away, the main portion higher on the bank left untouched. All future building was above the reach of high water.

British Columbia was speeding along with its mines and some of the biggest producers were having a hard time getting ore smelted and finished. One was the huge Le Rio operation just off the Rossland Trail and the owners decided to build a large smelter in Northport. Although the Canadians put up a spirited fight to have it on their side of the border it was plain the necessary materials for smelting, such as limerock for flux, existed in enormous quantities in Northport and the smelters could work the ore much more

BRICK TUNNEL at old Northport smelter which carried off gases and dust from furnaces.

OLD SMELTER AT NORTHPORT is in ruins, one stack standing, others having collapsed. International difficulties were headache during life of reduction works in U.S., mines in Canada.

HORSE TROUGH was scene of violence shortly after turn of century. Argument developed in saloon across street, one Penrose claiming another man, Jackson, owed him money. Jackson denied this and both "lickered up," tempers grew hot. Jackson drew his gun and Penrose fled across street behind watering trough. By this time he had his own gun unlimbered and when Jackson imprudently showed himself. Penrose "let him have it."

SCENE ON QUIET STREET in Northport shows old meat market in foreground. Next is town's notorious house of ill fame. Town had large proportion of single men who worked in mines and smelter and plenty of ways to spend their money were available.

cheaply there. The B. C. concern interested American capital and a U. S. company was formed to build the $250,000 smelter. The Northport Smelting and Refining Company plant was "blown in" in '97.

Labor troubles beset the company almost from the start. The owners bitterly resented any efforts of the Mill and Smeltermen's Union to organize the workers. In 1901 they went on strike, demanding they be allowed to join the union. The company retorted that any employee doing so would be fired and imported a large crew of non-union men from the east. As the strike continued sixty-two more men arrived and this started riots requiring the efforts of the Colville sheriff to quell. The strikers made things so tough for the new men, thirty-five quit.

At the end of nine months with nothing settled, the Western Federation of Miners with headquarters at Denver decided to cut the aid it had been extending to striking Northport men. One morning the strikers found the union's free eating place closed and many went hungry. A mass meeting was held, the strike called off, the union was abandoned and its charter surrendered.

Now international difficulties arose and for a time the smelter company was so harried it shut down entirely and the town became a ghost before its time. Accused of being aliens at the core, the company incorporated under the laws of Idaho and began accepting ores from the Coeur d'Alene districts in that state. Had the entire output of Kellogg, Mullen, Gem and other mines in that area been available to the Northport smelter the action would have meant a continuing life but the Idaho smelters took most of their ore. Once again the Northport plant closed down and the town was almost deserted.

There was a ray of hope when the rumor spread that the American Smelting and Refining Co. had bought the plant and people began to move in. Then the final, devastating blow fell, spelling Northport's doom. The buyers had no intention of opening the smelter. The machinery only was wanted and when this was moved out the source of Northport's life blood was an empty shell.

Today a large sawmill stands at the edge of the old smelter, taking up some of the employment slack. It is so close in fact, sawdust lies in deep drifts among the falling brick walls and cavernous roasting ovens. A large quarry working a fine quality of limestone-marble operates south of town.

BOSSBURG, WASHINGTON

Although twice in the history of the State of Washington the annual value of silver produced has exceeded that of gold, the yellow metal has held first place in the dreams of prospectors and the imaginations of those interested in old mining camps. The mines of Republic turned out millions in gold, those of Blewett Pass some, yet fully half of the old camps and ghost towns of the state have histories bound up with metals of another color.

Old Trinity was strictly a copper producing camp. The golden product of the Swauk district, including the Blewett Pass, was so alloyed with silver its color was definitely paled to a light yellow. The Ruby silver mines near Conconully were going full tilt in 1890 and at least a thousand miners were working in the camp at its height. The lead-silver mines of Colville produced large amounts of ore, the biggest being the old Dominion. For lack of roads or railroads the output was carried to Spokane at a cost of $100 a ton.

Five years later the Young America and Bonanza deposits were opened up at what is now called Bossburg, its first name Young America. The galena ore here was so rich some of it was "specimen" material and for some time the mines were going at top speed. The village grew up a short distance from the mines, just off the banks of the Columbia River.

The summer of 1892 saw 800 people at Young America and a quartz mill was erected. There were also stores, a good-sized school, the inevitable saloons and honkytonks. The next year the town was formally platted and rechristened Millington. A Congregational Church and large meeting hall were added and again, in 1896, the town was

ROTTING REMNANTS OF VEHICLES of another day lie in grass and weeds around old town.

CRUMBLING FALSE-FRONTED store in Bossburg had living rooms upstairs. Columbia River is just beyond, hills once heavily timbered with Ponderosa pine now show sparse cover.

rechristened—Bossburg in honor of the first citizen, C. S. Boss.

After mining operations tapered off Bossburg attempted to recoup its failing fortunes by establishing a ferry across the Columbia. Fruit orchards were set out and produced apples and pears, vines growing top quality berries. A sawmill had been put in working order and some lumber was shipped. The prevailing limestone formations were

tapped, stone was shipped in building blocks as were lime products.

None of these efforts lasted long. The old zip was gone, silver mining collapsed under the low prices and Bossburg died on the vine. Nearly all the old buildings are gone. A store, a few sheds, substantial schoolhouse still stand, the latter occupied by a family who had topped the old structure with a TV antenna.

"Alone? No!
...there was something else!"

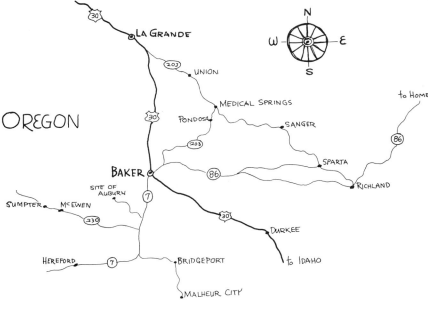

OREGON

AUBURN, OREGON

"Sweet Auburn! Lovliest village on the plain,
  Where health and plenty cheered the laboring
  swain."

These lines from the poem, "Deserted Village,"
inspired the naming of many towns and villages
in the eastern states and at least one in California's Mother Lode country. Then when a group
of restless prospectors from those diggings christened the first collection of shacks in the new Oregon gold fields Auburn was again a sentimental
choice. And prophetic enough, this Auburn has
long since been deserted and nearly vanished.

Early in 1861 a party headed by Henry Griffen
and his partner David Littlefield, on the way to
the Orofino diggings in what is now Idaho,
paused in Portland for rest and supplies. In one of
the bistros a man named Adams was loudly claiming full knowledge of the fabled Bluebucket Mine.
He referred to the tale of the Meek Party which in
1845 was said to have camped by a creek in
eastern Oregon while children of the emigrants
amused themselves picking up yellow pebbles in
a blue bucket. On the way again this dangled under the wagon for a while and then was lost. Later, on hearing tales of gold found in the mountains
the pioneers had a sinking feeling they had
likely overlooked a bonanza and now knowledge
of the place was gone. They remembered only
vaguely the stream, thought it probably a tribu-
tary of the John Day or Malheur Rivers.

Now here was a man claiming he knew the exact

location! Gold conscious Griffen and Littlefield,
imagination warmed by liquor, could not get to
the man fast enough. They engaged him to lead
them to the Bluebucket site in exchange for keep
and a percentage of the gold found. Setting out
in high spirits, the small party reached the arid
central portion of Oregon in good time and after
an extended rest, started for the location Adams
claimed to have pin-pointed.

Now the guide changed directions erratically.
Griffen and Littlefield thought little about it until
Adams made an about-face twice and told them
to camp in a dismal place without wood or good
water. After more uncertain movements, the partners had a conference, called a halt near the head
of Burnt River and demanded an explanation.
Adams was forced to admit he had not the slight-
est notion where they were or where the Bluebucket might be. The man was summarily sent
out of camp without food, arms or blankets and
told he would be shot if found following the party.
One soft-hearted member did get some food to him
to save his life.

Unable to agree on a traveling plan, the party
split, the majority deciding to retrace their steps
as nearly as possible. Shortly after crossing Blue
Canyon at noon, October 23, 1861, they reached
a good camping spot in a gulch. While Littlefield
shot some game and made supper Griffin sank the
inevitable prospect hole at the creek. Next morning they worked the hole further, panning when

HEADFRAME is only standing remnant of town, surmounts shallow mine. Hard rock mining was secondary to panning and sluice operations, amounting to so little usual piles of waste dumps are almost absent.

down to bedrock. Suddenly Henry Griffen was swirling and sloshing the sands faster and faster as though glints of the yellow metal were showing before the dross was poured off. When the residue came clear it was of such value excitement broke like a rocket. Pan after pan was finished with about a dollar's worth of dust in each, with even small nuggets here and there. At a feverish pitch the partners and others staked out claims, twenty-two that fateful day. Even the forlorn Adams, trailing at a discreet distance, was called up and allowed to peg out a claim of his own.

Four of the men—Griffen, Littlefield, William Stafford and G. W. Schriver spent the winter at the diggings, just able to build a cabin before a terrific storm blew up. With three feet of snow piled up, the weather suddenly turned warmer and rains melted the snow so fast flooding was general in the mountains and valleys. The men found they could not work without rubber boots and in the middle of December set out for Walla Walla for supplies.

They carried a poke full of Powder River gold dust which was not only accepted by merchants but sent by them to Portland and exhibited in a store window with a story that two men working on Powder River half a day had cleaned up two and a half pounds of gold dust! Almost by the time the four miners got back to the diggings a gold rush had set in. By spring thousands of gold-mad prospectors were panning every stream in the area. The ubiquitous William Packwood headed

RUINED STONE WALLS are sole remains of building in hell-for-leather gold camp of Auburn. Thickets of brush and weeds obscure site of town, once one of largest in Oregon. Living apple tree near ruins testifies miners sought respite from sowbelly and beans.

a group that laid out the town of Auburn on Blue Canyon Creek in April, 1862.

A population of 6,000 quickly made it the largest town in eastern Oregon and one of the largest in the state and it became the county seat in September of that year. It had all the trappings of boom town tradition—saloons, hook joints, dance halls. Murders and lynchings were part of it. In November of that action-packed first year miner Jack Desmond and gambler Henri Larabee became involved in an argument with an underworld character, Spanish Tom. The gambling debt quarrel simmered for several days and finally erupted in a shooting that ended with the deaths of Desmond and Larabee. The dead men were respected citizens where Spanish Tom was not and he was promptly snatched from custody to be strung up in a pine tree. All three victims were added to the growing population of Boot Hill. Next year Henry Griffen died at 59, was buried there. The stone now over his grave credits him as being "discoverer of gold in Eastern Oregon."

Auburn aged as rapidly as it grew, going into such a speedy decline its importance in 1864 was less than the upstart Baker, 14 miles northeast, and in June, 1868, a state election voted the county seat to that city. Sometime that spring the records were spirited away "very early one morning" and hauled to Baker in a wagon. Auburn citizens woke up to realize the town had reached the final step of ignominy, was fast headed toward oblivion and decay.

SITE of OLD AUBURN

ONE QUARTER OF A MILE NORTH OF THIS SPOT ON BLUE CANYON CREEK IS THE SITE OF OLD AUBURN, EARLY MINING TOWN AND FIRST COUNTY SEAT OF BAKER COUNTY FOUNDED IN APRIL 1862 AFTER DISCOVERY BY MEMBERS OF THE ADAMS PARTY. THIS WAS THE GOAL OF THE FIRST HISTORIC GOLD RUSH INTO EASTERN OREGON.

THE POPULATION AT ONE TIME WAS OVER 5,000 ONE OF THE LARGEST TOWNS IN THE YOUNG STATE OF OREGON

SIGN ERECTED 1941 WHITMAN NATIONAL FOREST. BY CO.B441 CCC

SIGN ERECTED BY C.C.C. BOYS marks nearest approach of good road, rocky track leading steeply down into Blue Canyon to few remnants of Auburn's heyday.

SPARTA, OREGON

At the southwestern edge of the snowy peaks in Oregon's Wallowa Mountains which nearly fill the northeastern corner of the state, is the Eagle Creek area of old mining camps. Here on a small "island" of granite in the center of a rather recent lava flow is Sparta, where in 1863, Squire Morris and his partner Neales Donnelly, made their Shanghai Gulch strike of small gold nuggets and dust in the stream gravels. A short time later Tom Koster made his find at the head of Maiden Gulch.

There was great excitement. These new finds were just what was needed to take up where the depleted mines of the area left off, and the town of Koster sprang up on the slope. Friends of the first discoverers renamed it Eagle City but authorities found the new name a duplication and the post office was established as Gem, after one of the larger mines. This was on August 7, 1871 and the name lasted over a year.

William H. Packwood, pioneer prospector, farmer, engineer and civic leader in Gem, proposed the town to be renamed in honor of his home town—Sparta, Illinois. Three other pillars of the community had home towns and weren't willing to

go along without a struggle. The four inscribed their choices on the sides of a square top and needless to say the side showing up was Sparta. Even if the others had heard of loaded dice, they accepted fate peaceably.

Sparta flourished. Gold dust up to $15,000 a week was sent through the mails, other large amounts by express and individuals. E. E. Clough and his father took $25,000 in dust and nuggets to Baker by horse and wagon.

But the water supply was inadequate for the placering equipment and Packwood backed a daring venture called the Sparta Ditch. Raising capital, he had the survey made and the 32-mile ditch built in two years. The placers had plenty of water but now the gold supply was thinning out.

With the richest mines abandoned, the Chinese workers from the completed transcontinental railroad moved in, content with placer gleanings. The luckless Orientals were harassed by wrathful whites, robbed, murdered and finally ejected. In 1915 all hard rock mining ceased and most of the shafts caved in. About two years later even the placering came to a stop.

SPARTA STORE only remaining business structure was solidly built to resist robbers. Erected in 1873 by W. H. Heilmer. 24x50'. Opening was celebrated with ball, attracting everyone in whole area, many from "metropolis" of 'Baker, 30 miles away. Store was operated for many years by Joseph Wright.

SANGER, OREGON

The little Wallowa Mountain community of Sanger, built on the flat just below the Sanger mine, and the mine itself, were originally named Hogum as a commentary on the nature of some of the earliest placer mines in the area. After the joke grew stale and the town sought a more dignified title, in 1871, the name of Augusta was selected, honoring Miss Augusta Parkwood, the first unmarried resident. After a year another change was made—to Sanger, the name of an early mine owner. The Sanger post office was established August 17, 1887, with William Aldersley the first postmaster. What the miners did for mail distribution for fifteen years, remains a mystery.

The Sanger mine on the road between Medical Springs and Lilly White was the largest producer in the district. The old placer camp operated for many years before the mine was started, yielding some half a million in easily obtained nugget and dust gold, separated from the granite gravels by panning, sluicing and Long Toms—when there was water. This was before ditches were so frequently constructed to bring water from Eagle Creek.

In 1870 the vein from which most of this loose gold came was discovered and named the Summit Lode. In 1874 this mine produced $60,000 from ore assaying $16 to the ton. A mint report shows it turned out $813,000 from '89 to '92. It closed in '97, opened for a short interval in 1900 then shut down for good with a total production of a million and a half.

The Sanger is on the west side of Eagle Creek and close to an older placer camp which had been a good producer. The Sanger had a long period of activity, closed for a time, opened again at the turn of the century, was then defunct. In 1915, the Oregon Almanac reported there were thirty people in the community. There was a little prospecting at Lilly White in 1930 with no result.

In the summer of 1936 there was a short reopen-

OLD SANGER HOTEL later occupied for many years by Charley Marks and his eighteen dogs. Cabin is placed in meadow among pines and deciduous trees of Wallowas. In summer wagons could be driven under upper floor for cool shade. In time of heavy snows sleighs were pulled directly to front door. In rear clear stream of cool water flows year around and spring house over it kept milk and perishables fresh.

ing of the Sanger. Baker druggist E. B. Cochrane with partner Harry Belden worked here all season but when the snow came to the Wallowas, they decided the results were not worth the effort and the mine died. The Wendts of Baker, its present owners, have placed a new roof on the old mill and hope to revive the workings when and if the price of gold goes up.

A large and impressive log cabin still standing on the flat below the mine has a varied and obscure history though it seems to have been a hotel at one time, the spring house just above the building being much too large to have served a private house. The first tangible story of it is, it was occupied for years by Charley Marks.

Old Charley graduated from Stanford, it is said, and went to Alaska with the gold rush using a dog team of Alaskan huskies. When he came to the Sanger cabin after the mines were down, he brought some of the sled dogs and bought others until he had eighteen. They all lived and ate with him in the house. On one of his rare visits to the biggest town in the area, Baker, he heard of a police dog which had bitten a child and might be destroyed. Charley brought the dog, Rex, home, made the huskies accept him, which they did after some fights.

The Wallowas see a heavy fall of snow every winter and Charley built up a complete dog team to haul a modified toboggan Alaska-style. In the winter trapping season he carried supplies to several line cabins and on one occasion he was following his marten traps when he came to an open spot in a frozen stream. There were several large fish

stranded here and Charley hankered to get one and change his diet.

As he walked out his snowshoes broke through the thin ice and he took a bad fall, his gun flying out of his hand and a bullet going through his knee. He crawled back to the line cabin, made a makeshift splint from a snowshoe and crawled on the sled. His lead dog was a veteran husky but the German shepherd Rex held the most important position, that of turning the sled. The dogs had been to the large Basin Mine workings many times and understood the word "Basin." Charley told them to head there and weak from loss of blood, blacked out. The timber was heavy and the snow deep but the dogs struck out and Rex carefully maneuvered the sled away from low-hanging branches. They reached the mine after several hours and the men there rushed Charley to a doctor.

He recovered from the ordeal with only a slight limp. He is 82 years old and lives in the same area at Keating. He has only four dogs now but they live with him in his little two-room shack and eat their bones there too.

VIEW THROUGH BROKEN WINDOW shows living room and fireplace of old log hotel.

ABOUT 100 FEET FROM LOG HOUSE is pile of beef bones where Charley Marks did butchering for dogs. Mr. Wendt of Baker, present owner of Sanger mine says: "I was out there once when I was a boy. It was in the summer and the smell from the pile of bones was pretty strong."

MALHEUR CITY, OREGON

There is a story that Malheur City received its name in the early days of mining there when a tunnel caved in trapping a French miner who died of his injuries. "Tam" McArthur, in his book "Oregon Place Names" thinks this is highly improbable, that the name came from the same source as did Malheur River. His version concerns Peter Skene Ogden, a Hudson Bay trapper, who made an expedition into the Snake River country and noted in his journal: "Tuesday, Feb. 14, 1826. We encamped on *River Au Malheur* (unfortunate river) so called on account of property and furs having been hid here formerly, discovered and stolen by natives."

As for Malheur City itself, it is not on the Malheur River but the much smaller Willow Creek close by and it was in this stream that gold was discovered in 1863. A group of miners who had left the exhausted El Dorado nearby, were prospecting for other diggings and made their find about the time they were ready to give up and go back to California.

The gravels of Willow Creek had plenty of gold and at first, when miners were easily satisfied, they panned and sluiced the stream when there was water in it and quit when there wasn't —which was often. Getting impatient at these enforced delays they made efforts to get water to the diggings and this resulted in the El Dorado Ditch, in that day an immense undertaking. The largest of its kind on the West Coast, it was planned and carried out by W. H. Packwood who engineered the Auburn and Sparta ditches.

The project was started in 1863 and was at first

FIRE LEVELLED ALL WOODEN HEADBOARDS in Malheur cemetery. Identification of these graves was lost, partially restored by memory, a few new markers erected. Some are pathetic in their brevity, such as: "A Mother and Her Three Children."

MANY YEARS HAVE PASSED over Malheur City since any mail was placed in box. Malheur is hot in summer, cold in winter and dugout style of home building had advantages besides making use of available materials. Rock and dirt walls had excellent insulating qualities, were only type to survive fire.

called the Burnt River Ditch since it was to carry water from that stream. The digging got off to a slow start but by '67 eleven miles had been built; forty-six more in the next two years. In 1870 the project was bought by an Illinois firm which speeded things up by putting 1,000 Chinese laborers on it. By some default the ditch was back in Packwood's hands in '74 and he kept at it four more years.

When the channel was carrying water it was 134 miles long and cut through many a big hill on its way to El Dorado and Malheur City, costing between a quarter and a half million dollars. An issue of the *Portland Oregonian* of that day report-

ed: "El Dorado Ditch in Baker County is now carrying . . . about 800 inches of water, from which is realized about $600 every 24 hours, over and above running expenses." This was below its capacity, as historian Isaac Hiatt wrote. "The main ditch was five feet wide at the bottom, seven at the top, with a carrying capacity of 2,400 miner's inches." But it was large enough to float logs for building purposes and proved to be a boon to Malheur City for five years, even if it did not pay for itself.

In 1887 Malheur County was formed and the town found itself out of Baker County and in the

FIRE IN 1957 started in tinder-dry grass, swept unhindered through Malheur, destroyed all wooden buildings remaining from mining heyday.

extreme northern end of the new one. El Dorado was dead, placer mining unproductive there and going out in Malheur. The ditch was no longer used by miners and its owners tried to find new uses for it. In 1911 the Eastern Oregon Agricultural Co. was formed to convert it to irrigation purposes but Baker County farmers were not willing to share the water with those in Malheur County and the costly project was dropped. And as the ditch dried up, so did Malheur City. On August 16, 1957 a disastrous grass fire devastated the few lingering remains of the town.

RICHMOND, OREGON

In 1889 a number of ranches were settled in the rolling sage-covered hills of Wheeler County, Oregon. Ranchers had to go all the way to Mitchell, about 19 miles to the south, or to Spray, about the same distance north, for their supplies. Their children were growing up without education except a little home instruction and many of the settlers felt the need of public worship. A meeting was held in one of the farmer's homes to see what could be done about a population center.

Among the earliest settlers here were the Gil-

liams, Donnellys, Keyes and Walters. These families attended the meeting as did several interested men from nearby communities, representatives of the cattle firm of Smith and Waterman from Waterman Flat and Caleb N. Thornburg who ran stock at Spanish Flat in the John Day area, was receiver of the land office at The Dalles and for whom the little community and post office at Caleb were named.

The meeting was successful in establishing plans for a town and all agreed the first building would

OLD COMMUNITY CENTER almost swamped by sagebrush and poplars. Starting as a residence, building expanded into general store, post office with T. B. Elrod as first postmaster, and general cracker barrel meeting place.

be a school. The name for the new city was not so easily settled, the effort almost breaking into hostilities. R. N. Donnelly and William Walters disagreed over the school site, Walters objecting to everything Donnelly proposed. Even the Civil War got into the controversy and Donnelly called Walters "Jeff Davis" because of his rebellious tendencies, vowing that if things ever did get ironed out the town would be called Richmond after the capitol of the Confederacy. When tempers cooled, Donnelly donated three acres of land for the school. And the name of the town agreed upon? Richmond.

Construction of the small schoolhouse was started as soon as lumber could be hauled to the site. This had to come from the sawmill at Six Shooter owned by E. M. Howell. A store was built and immediately prospered, people coming from many small outlying communities such as Waterman to trade at the new Emporium. Next was the Meth-odist Church and a large I.O.O.F. Lodge Hall. Other buildings followed and Richmond was a real town.

The biggest gathering ever held here was the get-together of the Wheeler County Pioneers. 450 attended and the festivities lasted a week. This was in 1901 and is still remembered by a few old timers.

Many factors contributed to the slow decay of Richmond. The "Tin Lizzy" and better roads made it possible for the farmers and cattle men to get to larger cities to buy their goods. The younger generation was not enthusiastic about ranching or the isolation involved and the older land owners died or moved away. Gradually the buildings were deserted and fell into disrepair, many collapsing or were burned. The few remaining ones, gray and shabby, present a picturesque and bona fide ghost town.

LONEROCK, OREGON

Scotland's greatest export is Scots and the newly married Spaldings were two of them, making the incongruous jump from the fishing village of Banff, Aberdeenshire, to the raw and bleak wilderness of Lonerock in 1898.

At 17, David Spalding went to the arid eastern section of Oregon to establish a ranch home for his intended bride, Sophia Essom, choosing the locality near Trailfork in an almost barren area of sagebrush and juniper trees. The nearest large settlement was Condon, some 20 miles away but a smaller one, Lonerock, was only five miles distant and David felt Sophia would not be too lonely with such near neighbors. After five years of improving the ranch he returned to Scotland and claimed his bride. She had been taking nurses' training, a skill of inestimable value in a land so far from doctors and hospitals.

On arrival at the lonely farm the young couple set to work in earnest to establish a few of the comforts, and these were few indeed. One deprivation was being almost completely cut off from the outside world. Both were eager for news from Scotland but getting mail was a chore. Their small home was some distance from the mail route and a temporary system was set up that gave the ranch its name. When the mail carrier came by the road intersection he would put the Spaldings' mail in a heavy paper bag and stuff it in the crotch of a large juniper. Before long the Spalding place was the "Paper Sack Ranch."

Sophia and David worked their place for a number of years, then moved to the comparative comfort of Lonerock. This town had been settled as a crossroads gathering place for ranchers and sheepherders and being on the main emigrant route a supply center was needed. Two ranch partners, R. G. Robinson and Albert Henshaw, laid out the town in 1881, seeing to proper platting the next year. Prior to this, in '72, a post office

TINY JAIL held last prisoner, drunken Indian, 25 years ago, once was crowded when sheep were moved to higher pastures by sheepherders who celebrated at crossroads settlement. After last tenant was freed, fire hose cart was moved in. Little shed at right held wood supply for stove. Just past corner of jail is seen edge of early hotel, the Williams.

was established, with Robinson carrying the mail from The Dalles in a buckboard or on horseback.

The arrival of the Spaldings was an occasion for rejoicing, both young people being popular in this new country as they were back home, and social life enjoyed a lift. Since David was an accomplished musician with accordion and piano, and Sophia with a pleasing voice, an entertainment group was started at their ten-room home with neighbors gathering in the evenings for songs and dances.

The couple had two children, Lovena and Cecil. Their mother would make a batch of cookies and leave the lid off for all nearby children to help themselves. She and David became close friends of the Robinsons, Hardies, Maddens and Campbells. Sophia's nursing ability stood her in good stead as she aided in many an emergency as unofficial midwife. She often helped a birth before the only doctor, overworked George Gaunt who might be miles out in the country, could get to the scene.

IMPOSING SCHOOL was once alive with children, even housed higher grades in one room 2 to 5 years ago, high school later moved to Condon. Sophia Spalding's daughter, Lovena Palmer, taught here between 1934 and 1942, another teacher, Ruth Potter. Only seven pupils remained in '60-'61 taught by Geraldine Overhulse. Old school is now entirely deserted, cupola still holding silent bell.

Busy as she was, Sophia planted a row of little trees along the side of the house and in dry spells carried water from the creek to keep them alive and pumped water from the well when the creek dried up.

People began to move away from Lonerock about the end of the first World War. Water was getting scarce to the point of crop failures every few years, the climate always rigorous, reaching 16 degrees below zero and 100 above. The Spaldings stayed on and even after David's death in 1935, Sophia kept the big house tidy and the front yard full of flowers, still administering to the needs of her dwindling neighbors.

In 1956 she fell, fracturing her hip, was taken to a Portland hospital. Upon recovering she stayed with her married daughter Lovena in Condon. Another fall two years later resulted in breaking her other hip requiring more hospitalization. From her wheelchair she cheered other patients as she ignored her own pain. In July of 1961 she died and was returned to the little Lonerock church for the funeral.

By this time the town was almost completely deserted but on that Sunday, July 29, the church was filled beyond capacity, more than three hundred people coming from far and wide to say goodbye to the woman who had held such an important place in their lives.

LONEROCK M. E. CHURCH dates from before turn of century, saw regular services for many years. Now worshipers gather only on rare occasions when minister of Assembly of God Church of Condon makes visit. Huge rock behind church gave town its name. Funeral services for pioneer, Mrs. David Spalding were held here.

WYOMING

CRESTONE
RAWLINS
WALCOTT
MEDICINE BOW
SARATOGA
CENTENNIAL
LARAMIE
RUDEFEHE
DILLON
BATTLE
RIVERSIDE
ENCAMPMENT
RAMBLER
BAGGS
COPPERTON

COLORADO

"Trees ... shrunken into shapes of desperation!"

RIVERSIDE, WYOMING

Riverside was never a mining camp but came into being as a gateway to the mining district and as a neighbor to the more important town of Encampment. Both resulted from the early days of barter from 1851 on. After the trading period ended and ranching started, a man named Dogget started a store and station, a few log cabins and shanties collected around it, the place taking the name of Dogget.

At the turn of the century the town had changed its name to the more fanciful one of Riverside and

boasted sixty buildings. One of these was a forty-room hotel which burned and was promptly rebuilt, a matter of questionable judgment as shady dealings of the big copper enterprise at Encampment caught up with the promoters. This with falling copper prices spelled the doom of the big hotel which reflected the whole of Riverside.

FORERUNNER OF MODERN HOUSE TRAILER Sheepherder's home had some "modern" touches—the truck wheels. Otherwise camper is typical of shelters used in past, well designed with many comforts, wood burning stove inside. Sheepmen were often suffocated at night with these overheating.

ABANDONED RANCH AT RIVERSIDE seems to typify popular conception of farmsite in wide open spaces. Central log building has false front—owner did blacksmithing in spare time. Goats from neighboring farm run loose.

ENCAMPMENT, WYOMING

On the stream later known as Encampment River, about nine miles above its junction with the North Platte, is a pleasant valley providing respite from the rough going in the mountains. Here prior to the '70s, Indians and trappers made common camp for the purpose of barter. Only tents and the flimsiest of shelters were needed in summer for temporary occupancy. The place became known as Le Grande Encampment.

About 1879 a number of minerals including gold and copper were discovered in the valley and a few settlers moved in. There was no stampede, the amount of gold small and no one was interested in copper. When the Nichols family arrived, with small daughter Lora, her father erected a one-room log cabin quickly before the bitter Wyoming winter set in. Two other branches of the family built their own cabins, to which was added the

Bagget's. Other settlers came and a thrice-weekly stage brought mail from Fort Fred Steele. Eventually a tiny post office and store were established at a point called Swan, four miles down the valley.

In 1897 Ed Haggerty found a copper mine and this was the start of Encampment as a town. Lora Nichols recalls that the first building in the raw settlement was the two-room log office of the mining company. The second was the hotel, also a two-story log affair, then a saloon to be followed eventually by twelve more.

Stage service was started from Saratoga to the north over roads of the most primitive types, barely passable in the deep spring mud, hub deep in summer dust and the worst conditions of all during blizzards.

"Then the wind would blow every which way," Lora recounts. "You couldn't see where you were going. When rumors began to fly that there might be a telegraph line to Encampment, father said it would be a good idea if only because of the poles, for in a blizzard a driver could at least find his way from one pole to another." When the snow got so deep the wheeled coaches could no longer force their way through the drifts, they were replaced by sleighs.

MASONIC BUILDING was originally erected in 1899 for Grand Encampment Herald, later shared by Lodge.

OLD PICTURE by Lora Nichols shows stage operating between Saratoga and Encampment in winter when sleigh was used instead of wheels. Peggy Dougherty was driving rig like this when he became lost in blizzard, was brought in by horse which knew where warm home stable was.

One of the best and most jovial of the drivers was Sam Dougherty. He loved to dance and was one of the first at the socials in the Encampment school. The three rooms would be made into one large hall by pushing back the big folding doors and everybody did square dances and reels. Women were scarce and Sam would grab another man for a partner and pretend he held a beautiful girl.

Until the bad blizzard Dougherty had never had any trouble driving stage. About the middle of December one bad winter, his sleigh was due and people started watching for him, had a good fire and hot toddy ready for him. The rig did not appear and the whirling, blinding gale of snow grew worse. Two hours later one of the horses came stumbling in, a mass of ice, dragging behind it the redoubtable Sam, his hands in a frozen grip on the animal's tail. Sam was unconscious and without help would have died.

Tough and sturdy, he survived although one leg had to be amputated and the hand that clung so desperately to the horse's tail was left with the thumb and only one finger. This would be the end of Sam's dancing, everyone thought, but he had a wooden extension fitted to the short leg and became "Peg Leg" Dougherty, and more affectionately,

MANY OF ENCAMPMENT'S original log houses survive, some covered by whipsawed boards.

"Peggy." And Peggy danced again too. When a square dance was held in the school house the next winter, Peggy was on hand. With a few toddies to get going, he danced with the best of them, singing his own composition: "The neighbors get sore when I dance on the floor, and make dents with my hic-hic-hickory limb."

The town of Encampment was built on shaky foundations. "Its promoters sold ten times the amount of stock they should have," said Lora Nichols. But while the boom lasted, the place, with 5,000 people, was one of the wildest and most boisterous camps in the State of Wyoming. A solid jail had to be built almost at the first, a log structure with a dirt roof, there being no shakes or shingles available, and prisoners had to be chained. A daily stage run was made to and from the railroad terminus at Walcott, one rig starting at Encampment and one from Walcott early in the morning, meeting at Saratoga. Later the railroad was extended to Saratoga and then came the big day when the Saratoga and Encampment Valley Railroad actually pulled into Encampment itself. The day of the stage coach was over.

The town had four newspapers at various times,

the one with the longest life, the *Grand Encampment Herald*, being established in a log cabin in 1898. Two years later it could afford a fine false-fronted building, later shared by the Masons who used the second floor. The *Encampment Echo* and *Encampment Record* had short lives, the *Valley Roundup* even shorter.

The first edition of the *Herald* came out on March 18, 1898, spreading "scare headlines" across the top of page one: "Grand Encampment, the World's Storehouse of Gold, Copper and Cobalt . . . the Coming Metropolis of the Rockies . . . Tangible Golden Wealth that Surpasses the Phantoms of the Klondyke." Banked below in only slightly smaller type: "Wonder of the Age, Grand Encampment has no equal on the globe, says Noah Siever. Days of '49 to be repeated in Wyoming. Thousands soon to take the trail."

The North American Copper Co. was formed and bought the main mine, the Rudefeha, for a half-million and sold thousands of dollars worth of stock. The company also bought and enlarged the smelter, building a fabulous tramway, longest in the world, to carry ore from the mine down to the reduction plant. Construction of it involved some intricate engineering, the tram's twenty miles of length crossing the Continental Divide. Its cables were supported by 304 towers, each bucket holding 700 pounds of ore, and it was capable of delivering 98 tons daily. During the five years after the sale of the mine in 1903, the town grew from a population of a few hundred to more than 2,000.

Encampment's first sign of trouble came in 1906, the year the concentrating mill at the big smelter burned. Two years later most of the remainder was destroyed. Yet for a long time the tram continued to dump its quotas of ore beside the ashes for a ready supply when and if the smelter was rebuilt. The railway came in 1908 but by that time the smelter was closed entirely, the price of copper having dropped. Now came legal troubles for the over-capitalized Ferris-Hagerty Company. It was accused of huge fraudulent stock sales and when this was proved in court, the company was finished.

Encampment continued to dwindle and in 1910 the tram was taken out. The railroad continued to serve the cattle shippers but trucks began to take that source of income away since they could go into the ranch yards and pick up the animals. For a few years more the railroad struggled along, its only job hauling finished lumber from the still-active sawmill near the gaunt station. When the lumber firm ceased operations, so did the railroad, its demise in June of 1962.

THIS WAS LAW, REAL ESTATE and records office of George Kuntzman. Little false-fronted structure is face-trimmed with light sheet metal. Plaque at right corners reads: "G. L. Mesker & Co., Evansville, Ind." Daughter of Kuntzman still lives in Encampment, s a y s: "I wouldn't have that little building torn down for all the world."

BATTLE, WYOMING

Battle was located almost at the summit of the Continental Divide which at this point is nearly 10,000 feet high. Snow lies on the ground most of the summer, the highland meadows lush with green grass while the lowlands are sear and yellow. This was also true in the wild days of Battle's height as a mining camp. The grazing land around the town was the best for cattle and the sheepmen cast their covetous eyes on it too. And so was provoked the classic hostility of the Old West. The sympathies of Battle lay with the cattlemen and anyone "smelling of sheep" was in danger of his life.

The camp had several saloons and in one of these, runs the legend, the notorious gambler Kid Blizzard was tending bar.

Normally wary sheepherders wanted their whiskey too and on a certain night a knot of them swaggered into the Kid's domain when he was in a particularly truculent mood. An argument soon started, Blizzard growing meaner by the minute as the boss sheepman taunted him about the girl friend who had left him the night before. At last the barkeep barked: "I wouldn't be so kind as to put the likes of you out of his misery all at once with a bullet" and brought the butt of his gun down over the needler's head. The victim staggered and managed to get his gun out, confusion taking over with everyone shooting, the cattle factions lined up against the sheep men. When it was all over Kid Blizzard lay bleeding, dead. The herder seemed to have survived since he managed to get out the door but in the daylight he was also found dead, slumped against the back wall of the schoolhouse.

The town's name of Battle did not come from this one. A pitched fight between Indians and soldiers gave Battle Mountain its name which was passed to the settlement. When copper was found on the west slope of the Divide, starting the mine called the Doane Rambler, a town sprang up taking the name Rambler. These mines and ones at the Rudefeha diggings began to haul ore over the Divide and down to the smelter at Encampment and Battle was the strategic spot near the high crest for a stopping place.

The Main and Kinsella Hotels and rooming houses sprang up overnight. Four general stores, several livery stables conveniently close to the

BATTLE IN LATE AUGUST — only time snow is gone. Picture taken in 1907 by Lora Nichols of Encampment. Hump on horizon in center is where present road crosses Divide. Waters flowing in this direction reach Grand Encampment River, North Platte and Missouri. Creek on other side joins Savery Creek which runs into the Little Snake, Yampa and Colorado.

hotels, a barber shop and sawmill were operating in Battle at its height.

There was always snow around the town, the nights cold even in summer and snow banks persisted in shady places. The rest of the year it lay so deep it was often necessary to dig tunnels to reach the doors of business houses. And the deep snows caused many avalanches. In 1903 two telephonemen lost their lives when swept over a cliff.

Miss Elizabeth Pettingill started a men's apparel shop. David's Dry Goods Emporium and Sol Funk's General Merchandise flourished. The *Battle Miner* reported news of shootings and optimistically talked up the rosy future of Battle as a metropolis. The girls of the several "houses of joy" didn't need to advertise their wares, they were placed conspicuously on the main street. They were not too choosy about customers but voiced a few complaints to the sheepherders when they found sheep ticks in their beds in the morning.

When the Ferris-Hagerty boom collapsed, so did Battle, and by 1907 everybody had moved away. Final disintegration came when CCC boys were instructed to burn the old historic remnants. A sign marks the spot now, careful scrutiny of the ground revealing old timbers and bottles.

SITE OF BATTLE is filled with snow on 4th of July when picture was taken. Town lay near Continental Divide at nearly 10,000 feet.

PICTURE TAKEN from same spot as one by Lora Nichols 55 years earlier shows same stumps, same horizon but no town. Some second growth timber has covered site sparsely, trees making slow growth in short season at this altitude.

RAMBLER, WYOMING

At the height of the western slope of the Continental Divide where the creeks start for the Colorado River, a vivid green hollow nestles in an alpine setting, a clear blue lake in its center. Around it tall, slimly tapered firs stand like candles and encircling the basin are snow-crested mountain peaks. Near the lake, in a forlorn huddle, are the few remnants of the activity that was Rambler, only two or three buildings still standing of the once bustling city and these sinking fast into the ground saturated by melting snows.

Here was a copper boom town attended by hundreds of people who built scores of stores and houses and through whose efforts half a million pounds of copper were produced up to January 1, 1904. Several carloads of this ore averaged more than half pure metal.

All this ore had to be hauled by mule teams up the steep pitch enclosing Rambler, over the Divide and down to Encampment smelter. Along the route and in the immediate vicinity were several other camps, most of them gone now, a few with paltry piles of rubbish and a beam or two to mark the sites.

Dillon was one, built for pleasure. Liquor was forbidden at the mine but no miner was expected to do without his favorite beverage. To take care of the situation, Malachai W. Dillon, a former soldier under General Crook, opened a house where a man could get anything he wanted by way of diversion. Meals were free to those who drank at the bar. Mary Lou Pence and Lola M. Hosmer, in their book—"Ghost Towns of Wyoming," say of Dillon: "Hundreds of the miners liked the place and sank sturdy foundations under their outhouses to show they'd come to sit a while."

In fact Dillon's main claim to fame seems to stem from its privies. Until a few years ago the first landmarks visible on approach were some strangely tall and thin structures. On closer scrutiny these became outhouses, about twenty feet high, a special arrangement to allow for winter's deep snows.

Dillon hung on even after the copper bubble burst but when the hotel and store burned in 1915 it gave up. The old saloon keeper stared at the dusty bottles in solitude for two years and then departed for Saratoga. Dillon became a shade, along with Coppertown and Elwood which were also in the galaxy of stars that once sparkled around the central sun of Grand Encampment.

"LITTLE HOUSE OUT BACK" sinks to grave in own pit. Boards of walkway over soggy ground in basin around Battle Lake are still in evidence. Nearly circular valley is enclosed by snowy peaks of Sierra Madre Range. Mountains show many bare ridges where snow easily avalanched, particularly in spring when mass settled from weight of season's accumulation.

UPPER STREET on side of canyon shelters these sole remaining buildings of Rambler. Aspens have grown up around abandoned town after pines and alpine firs were cut for boards or firewood, provide "nurse crop" for reforestation by shading young evergreens.

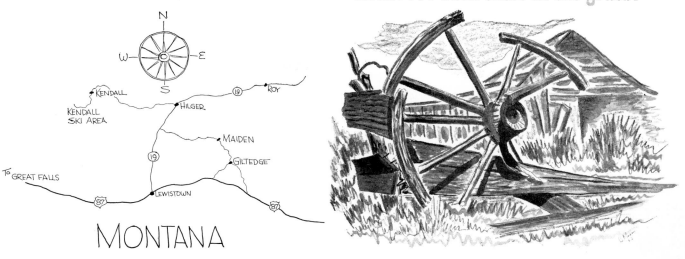

MONTANA

MAIDEN, MONTANA

The Judith Mountains of Montana are misnamed, according to legend. Meriwether Lewis of the Lewis and Clark Expedition wanted to make an impression on a certain girl at home by naming a mountain after her. He remembered her face better than her name. It was Julia.

First discoveries of gold in that part of the state were in the Judith Mountains. Partners David Jones and Skookum Joe Anderson — whose mother was an Indian, his father a Swede — had been grubstaked by Perry McAdow who was crowding them to produce something. Luckily they found a good showing of color in Alpine Gulch but unluckily winter was due. Sure enough, just after they started sluicing a hard snow put an end to all operations and the men had to wait out the winter on the open plain.

They barely made it back to their claim in the spring when a horde of hopeful prospectors who had heard the news began to arrive. One was a man named Maden and he was brusquely informed —"All this ground is taken up. Move on." Maden did move on, up the valley to another gulch which he named for himself and promptly put up a sign: "Camp Maden. Everybody welcome." The spot eventually became the center of a town, the word "camp" dropped from the name and an "I" added apparently by feminine influence, becoming "Maiden."

David Jones and Skookum Joe were ingenious as well as industrious. There being no boards in the gulch, they made sluice boxes by splitting trees into planks for troughs and in the bottom of each put a layer of clay. They ran the gold-laden gravels through these crude V-shaped channels, the heavier gold settling to the clay which was then removed, the gold separated.

This marvelous invention was not in use long for there came a revolting discovery—there was no more gold in the gulch, at least for easy taking. They turned to their backer, McAdow, who made an inspection of the vein in the rocks above the stream and hurried home to scare up more money. He had seen a good thing.

Maiden now came into an era of comparative prosperity. Instead of tree splitting, there were sawmills and boards and buildings went up in a frenzy. By 1883 there were 154 houses and stores in the town with six saloons and by 1888 the population had increased to 1200. Louis Berlanger opened a general merchandise store, taking in a partner until they disagreed too often, Berlanger going it alone and the partner starting another store.

Maiden had its ups and downs, its trials by fire and Indians. Fire took most of the town on several occasions and Indians would come around, ostensibly looking for buffalo but not overlooking animals of some resemblance to them—the miners' cows. Since these animals were hard to come by their loss was serious. In the winter of 1882-3 the Collan mill failed, throwing many out of work and owing several months' wages. The winter was severe and most of the dogs in camp were eaten. The military reservation at Fort Maginnis sent supplies to help out.

Then in 1883 a catastrophe of much larger proportions threatened the very existence of the prosperous camp. Maiden had been inadvertently built on the military reservation centered by Fort Maginnis, the fact studiously ignored heretofore. Like a bombshell came a notice posted in Maiden: "Order 26. All unauthorized persons now residing on the military reservation of Fort Maginnis, working in any mines, prospecting or carrying on any kind of business, are warned to leave the reservation forthwith, removing all property they may have built or acquired thereon. 60 days are granted for removal."

Reaction was immediate. A mass meeting was held August 9 in Dryden and Essler's Building, presided over by J. Beck, recorder for the Warm Springs Mining Co. The result was a lengthy petition stating the case of the beleaguered miners to the Post Commander, presented on the 11th. Capt. Durand read it carefully, then got out a map of the reservation. He decided that the army could not back down on its decision to remove all unauthorized persons from the reservation but he could, without too much trouble, cut off from the reservation that portion in which Maiden was situated. Maiden was saved.

BERLANGER'S DEPARTMENT STORE is in ruins as are most of buildings in Maiden, earliest of Judith Basin's mining camps.

ASSAY OFFICE was one of most important mining camp functions, had small chemical laboratory complete with retorts, ovens and other equipment for determining value of ore samples brought in by hopeful prospectors.

Perry McAdow had long since taken over the mine he had financed. As his share over and above what he already owned as the grubstaker, he had put in 20 gallons of whiskey and a stock of supplies from the sawmill he was now shutting down. This first big mine was known as Skookum Joe, later Spotted Horse after a friendly Indian chief. As the Spotted Horse the mine became famous throughout Montana. The Maginnis mine was also a heavy producer, the two accounting for about $10 million in gold.

About 1891 things began to go wrong at the mines. Complaints came from the stamp mills that the ore wasn't worth processing any more, the miners admitting the veins were pinching out. Rising costs cut profits so much, in view of the lower grade ores, they could not keep going. Maiden began to fail, the 1200 people faded to 200 in 1896 and more left until the town was entirely empty. But Maiden had given impetus to mining in the Judith Basin and its people had only to move over to newer camps like Kendall.

GILTEDGE, MONTANA

The history of this camp is one of repeated disappointments. The ores gave up their metals reluctantly, labeled "refractory," and while getting them out of the mine was easy enough it was quite another matter to make them pay. This gave rise to a most elaborate plan to disguise gold shipments.

The Whiskey Gulch mine produced well but the amount of gold obtained was so low the superintendent was ashamed of it. He kept the results secret also because some eastern investors were nibbling at an invitation to expand the finances of the operation. He reasoned that if he took the bullion to Billings for shipment to the mint rather than to nearby Lewistown, there would be no leak as to the skimpy production.

This he did and his secret was safe—but now he had another worry. By the grapevine the superintendent had heard certain unsavory characters in town had learned he was shipping the gold on his own, robbing the company at the same time, and they planned to hold him up on some lonely road. So he filled the bags with junk to weigh about the

WHEN JAIL FELL DOWN someone saved stout, barred window frames. Prospect of rebuilding hoosegow seems remote.

same as the bullion and labeled them for the mint as usual—and stashed the real article under the floor of his buggy. He made the next trip without being molested—and all subsequent trips. Whatever happened to the robbers he never knew.

The low ore content resulted also in a spectacular buggy race. The main mine, the Giltedge, was having a particularly bad time at the smelter. Results of the last roasting had been so poor the men didn't get their Saturday pay. They held their protests but when another week rolled around without pay, they revolted, inducing the sheriff to issue an attachment against the bullion ready for shipment.

The man in charge of the mine was Bob Ammon, a New Yorker, and he decided to get the gold to the station in Great Falls for shipment, in spite of the hold out. He loaded it into his buggy and headed out of town, but the watchful sheriff had been expecting some such move and started after him in his own rig. He caught up with Ammon but couldn't overtake him on account of the narrow road. His horse hung on the tail of Ammon's buggy all the way to Great Falls and up to the railroad station. Ammon jumped on the train and the sheriff grabbed his arm. But the New Yorker had his ace card. He had legal training and knew what to do. He smiled calmly at the sheriff and said: "You are now in Cascade County and out of your jurisdiction of Fergus County. Take your hands off me."

Giltedge had not attracted much attention before 1893. Even then nothing too spectacular happened but buildings began to go up and the aspects of a town began to appear. Next year the camp had its first school, young H. A. Moulton its first teacher although he himself had no education. He had a bad time with his "rough neck" pupils, some of whom were older than he was. Moulton wore glasses and came to school one morning to find each boy had shaped wires like spectacles across his nose. By sheer good sense and persistence he eventually won the respect of the pupils and taught the Giltedge school for years. Another young man, David Roberts, started a blacksmith shop, Wise and Co., and owned the butcher shop as well. Sanville Hurvitch was the first postmaster.

By 1895, when neighboring Maiden began to fail, some of the abandoned buildings were moved to Giltedge, one of them the hardware store owned by M. L. Poland. Poland had operated the store in Maiden almost from the town's inception and now all he could do was leave it to his son.

The store was moved to Giltedge on logs used as rollers and Norman Poland who had worked in

HOTEL OR BOARDING HOUSE has stark, lonely quality of old abandoned buildings, emphasized by Montana's "big sky." Giltedge's remaining buildings are scarce, creating open, gaunt look.

the store as a boy was now the manager. A large hotel was put up with a fancy bar replacing the first makeshift one which had a dirt floor. The town jail was substantial, with window bars set in wide casings installed after the first two sets had been pried out by jail-breaking drunks and horse thieves.

During the period of prosperity for the town, shortly after the turn of the century, there were 600 voters and a considerable total population, counting wives, children and the many transients.

The ores, refractory from the first, grew more so as the years wore on and when the biggest smelter failed, the camp began to shrivel. One enterprising miner, losing his job at the Giltedge mill, started a much needed industry, making fence posts to keep stock from wandering too far. The plant had a pool filled with preservative oils in which posts were soaked, running in and out of a crude tramway. The old operation is falling into ruin but today a new one is working, the only visible industry in the town.

KENDALL, MONTANA

In its heyday Kendall turned out a great wealth of gold, the bullion sent to Lewistown for shipment to the mint. There were plenty of road agents ready to appropriate it and plenty of subterfuges used to foil them. All three stage lines out of town were used without a set pattern. Sometimes a passenger would take the gold out in a trunk or it might be in a sack carried openly in a buggy. The ruses were so many and so varied it took a sharp bandit to locate the gold. About all he could count on was the signal. When the smelter was finishing off a batch of bullion in the final "roasting," there would be a roaring noise announcing to all and sundry another load of gold would soon be on its way.

On one occasion a large shipment of about $50,000 was to be sent in to the bank. The stage driver was instructed to take the bag to Brown's Clothing Store instead, when he got to Lewistown, which he did. Brown was busy with a customer but told the driver: "Just leave the bag on the counter.

I'll put it in the safe later." But his streak of brisk business continued and when closing time came he forgot the gold, leaving it on the counter. That night several men who had got wind of the shipment and knew where it would be delivered, broke into the clothing store and blew open the safe. They did get $200 but the gunnysack of gold remained safely and securely on the counter.

In the early days of mining the practice of "salting" was quite common. Kendall had some experts in this line and one of them planted some rich ore in the mouth of a worthless mine and took in an unwary buyer, one Barnes. This man was eager to be a mine owner and didn't look beyond the samples in front, yet was cautious in another respect. As soon as the first deal was closed he staked his three sons-in-law to claims around his mine to protect any extension of the vein. After working the mine for several months he finally decided he had been flimflammed and turned a few desultory efforts toward one of the protecting claims. The

RUINS OF FIRST PRESBYTERIAN CHURCH stand on hill slightly off street surrounded by second growth trees mostly pines.

BANK AT LEFT shows large square vault in center of ruin. Large department store is nearly gone — evidence of both buildings fast disappearing due to vandals carrying stones away.

INSIDE WALL OF DEPARTMENT STORE shows where stairway paused at landing. Lath and plaster covered walls, concealed more handome stone.

result—over $2 million in gold in the next few years, the huge Barnes-King operation.

The first really good mine at Kendall was the Goggle Eye, so named from the way the discoverers looked at the first sight of the gold. It was worked by George Mason but he couldn't stand the expense of getting it started so turned it over to Joe Wunderlin and Bob Woodman. That was about 1899 when Kendall began to boom and several buildings were erected. One of these was a boarding house with a restaurant on the ground floor, owned by Harry Kendall who at that time had no special interest in mining. But the all-absorbing lure of quick riches got him too and he invested some of his boarding house money in a mine just getting started and whose owners needed capital for expansion. He worked his investment up to $450, enough at this stage for the controlling interest. The mine paid moderately but still needed much more money to realize its potential.

Kendall approached Finch and Campbell, mining promoters of Spokane and they were interested enough to send a man to look it over. Kendall was asking $50,000 for the mine and this stopped them. Then one of their experts, a man named R. K. Neal, looked it over on his own and recommended its purchase by the firm. By this time the mine was doing better and Kendall raised his price to $450,000 with a royalty of 10% on the profits. The deal went through and Kendall went back to his boarding house. The mine boomed into heavy

production, Kendall's 10% paying him more than a fortune before it was all over.

One interesting point about the ores at Kendall was "no one ever saw the gold in them." The metal was so finely divided it was never visible in the raw state. Therefore Kendall's refining methods required the cyanide process, one of the first camps to employ it.

The ore was first crushed into fingernail-sized pieces, a strong solution of cyanide run over it. Cyanide was extremely dangerous and there were many narrow escapes from death in the mines and mills. The cyanide dissolved the gold and the mixture was then added to zinc shavings which precipitated the gold, the resulting black sludge roasted in a furnace. When the zinc was driven off the gold was left.

The big cyanide mill started off with 40 men but soon expanded to 194. By this time the town had several pretentious stores, a large bank, two churches and its trade by mule teams and freight lines was a contributing factor in the growing economy of Fergus County.

Kendall was the last mining camp of consequence in the area, its combined mines turning out more than $6,400,000. When they were exhausted the town went into decay rapidly, the demise speeded up by the fact that many mine tunnels ran under the buildings so they later sank into the ground. There is not a habitable structure there now, only gaunt stone ruins through which cattle wander at will.

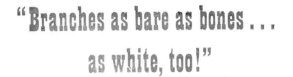

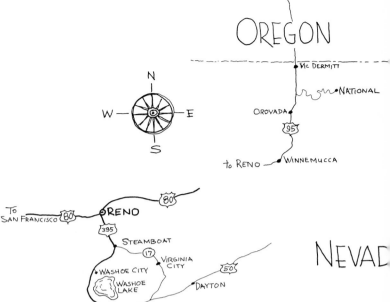

OREGON

McDermitt

NATIONAL

Orovada

95

to Reno — Winnemucca

80

To San Francisco 80 — Reno

395

Steamboat

17 Virginia City

50

NEVAD

Washoe City

Washoe Lake

Dayton

Carson City

395

NATIONAL, NEVADA

CABIN HAS LONG LACKED human tenants but birds have made themselves at home.

What is left of National is in the Humboldt National Forest. The area was classed, in a time of rich bonanzas, as one of the richest. Its ores contained many "jewelry store specimens," a term used to describe chunks of quartz in which gleamed solid nuggets of gold. The National mine alone produced more than $8 million.

National had a short life but a merry one. Ignored by prospectors in Nevada's early gold discovery period, it did not come into its own until the period called "automobile prospecting days." As evidence that the time of the burro had passed, two of the places named around National were Auto Hill and Radiator Hill.

Soon after the first discoveries of gold on the site by J. L. Workman, blocks of land were leased and the place became a beehive of real estate activity as well as the essential mining. In 1909 the Stall brothers ran into the National vein 40 feet down. Much of the ore removed from it assayed out at $75 per pound, the bulk of the shipped ore $24 per pound and tons were discarded with a value of $2 per pound.

With ore so rich "high grading" was carried on by many of the miners. It is estimated the National alone lost more than a million to these thieves. The worst of it was the citizens seemed to regard the

MANY ATTEMPTS WERE MADE to steal thunder of big National mine, prospectors constantly gophering in hills with small, individual diggings. few of which panned out. Cabin and small dump are evidence of one.

DO NOT DESTROY
HOOK DOOR
WHEN LEAVEING
LEAVE THINGS
ALONE

"REASONABLE REQUEST" is scrawled on door of miner's cabin in National.

practice of smuggling out "blossom rock" as being quite legitimate. The company had a hard time prosecuting the occasional miner who was caught at it, public sympathy being with the culprit. Discharging the guilty one only resulted in reprisals by the other miners, sometimes known to blast a tunnel after their safe exit. Even though lunch boxes were searched nuggets were often concealed in body cavities.

During the period of greatest activity the only law in National was that of the company which played searchlights on the mine at night and posted a 24-hour guard around it. But the company didn't give a hoot what the miners did off duty. The one long and narrow street winding up the canyon was lined with a concentration of "houses" bent on ex-

tracting everything a miner had earned or stolen. Such activities weren't always painless, many a man rolled or even killed for his wages.

One of the largest honky tonks stood just above the National mine. It boasted a second story with a hall down the middle between the cubicles where the girls took their customers. Downstairs a grand piano tinkled out its tunes, a long bar at the right sported large plate glass mirrors and mahogany fixtures. Out in back were two tall, narrow structures separated slightly, one "his" and one "hers." Now the house of pleasure has fallen flat and all of its fixtures have decayed away except the frame and wires of the piano. Still standing are the two little "Chick Sales."

WASHOE CITY, NEVADA

Young George W. Derickson, editor of the three-months-old *Washoe City Times* had been getting away with murder in his editorials. This wasn't unusual in the Old West of the 1860s when editors printed exactly what they thought without restraint or fear of libel suits.

Subscriber H. F. Swayze had sent in "a letter to the editor." Derickson printed it and wrote a sarcastic story about it. As soon as the offending issue was on the street the angry Swayze went to the newspaper office and demanded to see the editor. Derickson attempted to soothe the seething Swayze by telling him his printed comment had only been the truth, a remark not calculated to do any soothing.

The heated argument ended in a duel out on the street, both men firing at the same time. Both bullets found their marks, fatally in the case of editor Derickson. Swayze received a shattered jaw and

three years in the Nevada State Penitentiary just out of Carson City.

Washoe City had come into being because it had what was needed elsewhere. The spot where it stirred into life is at the foot of Mt. Davidson on the one side and the High Sierra on the other. Virginia City on top of the hill was suffering for lack of lumber which had to be sawed out of timber from the Sierra slopes from where also its water came. Its ore also had to be sent away for smelting. And so Washoe City sprang up to serve its more glamorous neighbor, the fabulous Virginia City. Timber was hauled down from the high mountains and whipsawed in Washoe. Water was piped in a gigantic syphon from the crystal-clear streams in the Sierra through Washoe where maintenance crews were quartered. And silver ore also came down to it from Virginia City to be smelted.

All this began to happen in the winter of 1860-

BANK AND WELLS FARGO BUILDINGS had iron doors and shutters similar to those in use in gold country on other side of Sierra in California. Photo was made in 1955. Both structures have since fallen to ground.

LAST BUILDING REMAINING in old Washoe City in 1962. It stands at right of sites of structures shown in other Washoe picture. Fringe of bricks can be seen adhering to edge of stone building.

61 when the first buildings were put up. By 1864 when several sawmills were feverishly turning out lumber for the booming Virginia City there was a population of 2,500. Smelters belched smoke from fires which were consuming the Jeffrey pines of the Sierra and refining huge quantities of silver ore coming down the slopes of Mt. Davidson on the Virginia and Truckee Railroad.

When slow death came to the mining camp in the clouds, Washoe City likewise expired, its reason for existence gone. Old Washoe's last shred of dignity was wrested away when in 1871, the upstart Reno, which had sprung up a few miles north, took over as the seat of Washoe County.

More substantial than Washoe City itself is the nearby imposing mansion of Sandy and Ella Orrum Bowers. The couple had started married life almost penniless in the mines on the fringes of Virginia City, then made millions from small investments in mining stock. They spent the money madly, had the huge house erected, to be ready on their return from a trip to Europe. They didn't enjoy either their wealth or their mansion for long. Sandy died at thirty-five, his widow lost all the money and the house, dying a pauper in 1903. The two with their daughter are buried on the hill a short distance behind the house.

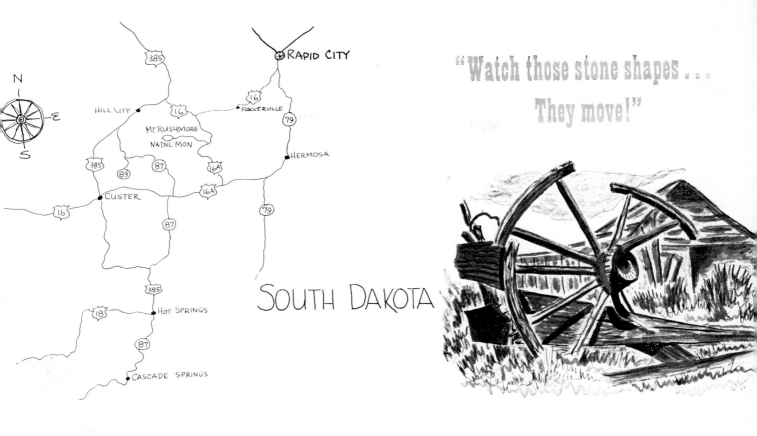

"Watch those stone shapes . . . They move!"

SOUTH DAKOTA

HILL CITY, SOUTH DAKOTA

Hill City is the second oldest camp in the Black Hills. Custer was settled first and just to be different, Hill City started with gold, then found rich deposits of tin.

With the gold discovery the first tents were put up in Hill City in the fall of 1875. Winter put a stop to any solid construction and spring brought the big news of the bonanza at Deadwood. Everybody in the infant camp left for the new diggings—everybody but one man and his dog. This lonely pair kept the vigil until the end of summer when a few disgruntled prospectors returned from Deadwood. Again it was too late for permanent building and the little group huddled in tents through another rugged winter.

Next spring saw an influx of people, prospectors and ranchers attracted by the fertile soil in the valley. Placering was extended to more distant points on the creek and a good ledge of gold-bearing quartz was located.

All this was according to gold camp pattern. Then suddenly affairs shot off at an angle. Tin was discovered close to Hill City. One legend has it a Dr. S. H. Ferguson was operating his mica mine, the Etta, when he came across the vein of tin. Not

recognizing the metal, he supposed it to be silver, getting the truth when it was assayed. Another version asserts two early day "rock hounds", George Coats and Joe McClure, were out in the hills herding their cows when they came across a chunk of cassiterite, recognizing it from a piece in their collection. They staked claims and formed a company.

The facts begin with an English syndicate forming a corporation of English and American stockholders—Harney Peak Consolidated Tin Mining Co. It bought up all areas in the district resembling the spot where the tin ore had been found, spending over $5 million. Their plant was set up and put into operation. The future looked secure, the vein rich in the valuable tin. Yet in a few months the bottom fell out of the project with internal strife and a diminishing supply of good ore.

This was a severe blow to the camp but gold mining was still going on to sustain it for a number of years. It was permanently saved by becoming a center on the railroad, kept alive by tourists attracted to a collection of old trains, one of which makes a daily sightseeing trip.

175

WHEN THIS VINTAGE MODEL came out it was considered the very latest thing. One big advantage was front window in cab enabling engineer to look straight ahead instead of leaning out side. Another improvement was taller stack, giving better draft for burning raw lump coal.

EARLY MODEL ENGINE from Lima Locomotive Works, dated in '80s, was used in later years as switch engine. Switchman rode on little platform (lower center) called foot board. When he coupled cars in building up train, he lifted iron bar above and left. Action raised extension at right, pulling up chain which released coupling which in turn locked into similar device in wanted car. Mechanism also hooked on to snow plow for clearing yards.

MAIL CAR (at rear) was traveling post office. Built in 1880 by Pullman Co., it was in service from 1883 to 1938 for Denver, South Park and Pacific, then for several years on Colorado and Southern between Denver and Leadville carrying millions in silver and gold bullion. Engine was called Chief Crazy Horse, was operated by Deadwood and Central, bore old time cow catcher. Windows on right side of cab were used by engineer to scan tracks ahead. When fireman was not shoveling coal he looked from left side. Water tank is immediately back of cab, was filled from water tower by let-down pipe.

CUSTER, SOUTH DAKOTA

The Sioux had known about gold in the Black Hills. They had shown samples of it to Father De Smet even before prospectors sneaked into that section against government orders. The rumors of golden wealth in the streams of the Hills not only persisted but expanded to fabulous proportions.

By the terms of a treaty made with the Indians in 1868, the Cheyenne Sioux were given the Black Hills to have and to hold forever. The white man couldn't use the rough terrain for farming or any other foreseeable purpose so he could afford to be "generous." The Indians were reasonably well satisfied; there was plenty of game and many good streams for fishing. But they thought, since this was to be their last stronghold, they should be left undisturbed. Gold being what it is and men being what they are, they were not left alone. The very next year saw a chain of events leading to the massacre of Custer's army, huge-scale gold mining in the Black Hills and the removal of the Indians from the land given them.

Charley Collins played a part in this drama. He was an Irishman who yearned to remove the British yoke from his countrymen. He had a patriotic compulsion to establish a branch of Fennin Society in the Black Hills where the members could accumulate piles of gold, gain enough strength and courage to march on Canada. His Irish paddies could overthrow the British there and eventually lick Britain herself. To stir up interest and support for his fanatical scheme he wrote sensational pamphlets about the fortunes waiting in the Black Hills. . . "mountains of pure gold lie concealed in the pockets and crevices. It can be picked up with bare hands in a thousand bubbling streams of mountain water." Such inflammatory fliers started plans for an expedition into the Black Hills to set up an Irish colony.

Before the Irish brigade got started however the U. S. Army, protecting the rights of the Indians, stopped any movement. Instead, it organized one of its own, ostensibly to find a better connection to Fort Laramie in Wyoming. On July 2, 1874, General George Custer left Fort Abraham Lincoln with 1,000 men. The procession included a brass band, hundreds of supply wagons, cook outfits and spare horses, a string of cattle following for slaughter purposes. As soon as the train reached the Black Hills the men began to pan the streams, as though this was the way to find a new route. In August the party had reached a campsite at the place where the town of Custer was later established.

The first day in camp two of Custer's men, H. N. Ross and W. T. McKay, panned the waters of

LINE OF LITTLE STRUCTURES left over from Custer's early day stands in path of "progress" and faces destruction. At left is lumber yard dating from days when Black Hills were covered with tree cutters as well as gold seekers. Next is old firehouse which sheltered little hose cart, Custer's only protection against fiery disaster. Next is first school house. One teacher taught all eight grades in one room, the few pupils in each class coming forward in turn.

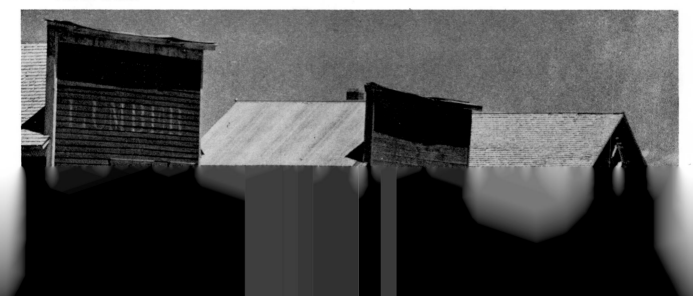

SECURELY BARRED WINDOW of little stone jail located in back of fire station in old section of Custer. It became needed in earliest days but almost all manpower was out in the hills and only one man, a confirmed drunkard, was available. He claimed to be an expert stone mason and was hired to build jail, being watched closely to see he didn't get a bottle. Toward end of job (section shown here) construction looked haphazard. When builder was paid off at end of work, he bolted for the saloon, became so boisterous and abusive he had to be hustled off to the new jail as its first occupant.

French Creek with such interesting results Custer wrote to his command: "I have upon my table 40 or 50 particles of gold about the size of the head of a small pin and most of it is from a single panful of earth. In one place the miners reported they found gold in the roots of the grasses. It has not required an expert to find gold in the Black Hills. Men without previous experience in mining have discovered it with little expense of time and labor."

Such a report (actually made public by the War Department) was not calculated to suppress gold talk or any plans to go to the Black Hills. Collins, made bolder by the activity, reorganized his expedition and made a settlement in the Hills. He had hardly got inside the stockade when an army detachment escorted the group of men and a woman named Annie Tallent back to their homes. The return trip was a little easier for Mrs. Tallent in that she rode on the broad back of a mule instead of walking.

However such attempts of the army to stop prospecting was futile. Gold-hungry hordes infiltrated the Hills until the area was thrown open to mining and homesteading. The army even sent detachments to protect the prospectors and settlers.

The camp, first called Stonewall in honor of Stonewall Jackson, was renamed Custer a month later and laid out by a townsite company in July, 1875. Plans had been made for the new town at a miners' meeting on French Creek. Actual "surveying" was done by a Tom Hooper with a pocket compass and two lengths of picket rope. Streets were made wide enough for teams to turn around. 1,400 buildings were put up during the first hectic three months and in less than a year the population had soared to 6,000.

No one dared a foray beyond the edges of town without protection. Indians were lurking near every tree and rock. Any horse or cow straying away a few feet immediately vanished. Often bolder groups of savages made sudden raids on the town and took all the stock they could find. Settlers and prospectors arriving in Custer told of ambush and sudden death. To offset such dangers a group of 125 citizens was organized under Captain Jack Crawford, known as "Custer Minute Men" and did reduce the number of Indian attacks.

With gold in the past, Custer has found other means of support. It is situated on a highway crossroads and is by no means dead, though not the roaring camp it was. The old is mixed with the new and Custer treasures its past.

CASCADE SPRINGS, SOUTH DAKOTA

Hot Springs, South Dakota, lies at the extreme southern fringe of the state's famed Black Hills. To the south stretches the Saw Tooth Range and on the east is Battle Mountain, forming a beautiful natural basin. The area is further endowed with springs pouring forth waters in abundance which are reputed to possess many health giving properties. Before 1879 when the first white settler arrived, Indians made pilgrimages to bathe in the springs. By 1881 a town had sprung up. People came to the springs and stayed to farm, raising provender for other health seekers.

A few miles south of this popular Hot Springs was a similarly situated valley close to the beautiful Cheyenne River. This spot also had a gushing spring, a veritable fountain pouring forth its waters so enthusiastically they formed a good-sized stream. But Cascade Springs was only a name,

DETAILS OF ALLEN'S BANK revealed by telephoto lens. Glass windows have long since disappeared, boards substituted to keep weather out, interior dark but fully equipped. Ruins of church are across street.

IMPOSING GROUP OF GAUNT BUILDINGS stands in lonely majesty at side of Cascade Springs. Left is Allen's Bank built of native stone. Next brick structure was store for general merchandise. Brick construction seems solid in front, is falling away from underlying whipsawed boards in rear. Frame building was next, now gone, at right curious combination of saloon and bowling alley.

with no resorts, no reputation. In fact only one man, a resident of Hot Springs, knew much about the place, having hunted in the area and bathed in the springs. He was apparently an opportunist for when he heard by grapevine a railroad was to pass close to his favorite bathing spot, he visioned a great health resort of his own.

He kept his plans to himself as long as he could. Making discreet inquiries of the agents of the proposed railroad—Chicago, Burlington and Quincy, he was told the rumors were correct. So in the year 1888 things began to happen at Cascade Springs. The promoter seems to have had no trouble interesting big money, this in the person of a Mr. Allen. This gentleman's faith was great. He not only put funds in the project but built a bank in the settlement, a structure of native stone so imposing it looked like a castle with turreted battlements.

Also built of the native pinkish stone was a huge hotel. It was nearly a city block long, had three stories surmounted by an octagonal tower, making an imposing sight on the sagebrush bare ground. Erected next was a frame building for a general merchandise store. Just South of this rose a hybrid. Primarily a bowling alley, it had a ramp running up to double doors big enough to admit a horse and buggy. The driver could then step over to the bar to remove the dust from his throat and proceed leisurely to the business of bowling. The main building was not long enough to permit an alley of proper length so an extension was added to the rear, an elongation which lends a very strange look to the building as it stands.

Next came the bath house. This was intended to outdo the one at Hot Springs and it did in at least one respect—the tubs were of solid marble. There were plans for the usual quota of saloons sufficient for an expected population of two to three thousand and two were actually built. And the builder had such an unerring knowledge of human nature he put up a lavish brothel near the bath house.

Curiously, amid all this spending of money and hectic construction, no one seems to have checked on the coming of the railroad. When the news did come it was devastating. The whole town was shocked. The railroad was indeed building, not to Cascade Springs but through the town of Edgemont, a hated neighbor and rival.

The town so full of promise could not cope. It quietly curled up its well-bathed toes and died. Most of its buildings had never been finished, others never occupied. The big hotel was a shell with no furniture, the bath house never ran water into its marble tubs. Today few people, even in South Dakota, have ever heard of Cascade Springs.

CUSTOMER OF BOWLING ALLEY was offered every convenience, could drive buggy up ramp into saloon. Extension at rear provided sufficient length for alley. Upstairs, fancy dormer embellished establishment indelicately referred to as "cat house."

LIVERY STABLE is over city block long, would hold many horses and rigs.

REAR OF BOWLING ALLEY shows extension of lane.

THE ROLL CALL OF THE SHADOWS

A ROSTER OF KNOWN GHOST TOWNS

Publisher's note: This listing makes no pretense of being complete. As this is being written both Mr. Florin and Dr. Mason are in the field photographing and researching the material for additional works to supplement, "Western Ghost Towns," the first of this series, and this book "Ghost Town Album" the second.

Towns in large type are treated either in "Western Ghost Towns" or "Ghost Town Album" as indicated. Those in small type are candidates for future publications and are listed for the benefit of the reader who may wish to investigate them himself.

ARIZONA

Western Ghost Towns	Ghost Town Album
Chloride	Tombstone
Goldroad	Gleeson
Oatman	
White Hills	

Jerome, McMillan, Pearce, Crown King, Mineral Park, Charleston.

CALIFORNIA

Western Ghost Towns	Ghost Town Album
Ballarat	Mariposa
Bodie	Hornitos
Cerro Gordo	Bear Valley
Darwin	Sawmill Flats
Masonic	Columbia
Swansea	Sonora
Calico	Jamestown
	Jackson
	Vallecito
	Murphys
	Altaville
	Mokelumne Hill
	Volcano
	Fiddletown

Coloma, Placerville, Nevada City, Downieville, Whiskeytown, Shasta City, Randsburg, Weaverville, Panamint, Hobo Gulch.

COLORADO

Western Ghost Towns	Ghost Town Album
Animas Forks	Cripple Creek
Eureka	Victor
Gladstone	Lake City
Kokomo	Bonanza
Leadville	Villa Grove
Saint Elmo	Crestone
Silverton	Creede

Central City, Black Hawk, Apex, Silver Plume, Georgetown, Fairplay, Alma, Breckenridge, Ward.

IDAHO

Western Ghost Towns	Ghost Town Album
Burke	Leesburg
Gem	Shoup
Idaho City	Bay Horse
Murray	
Pioneerville	
Placerville	
Potosi Gulch	
Silver City	

Bitch Creek, Bonanza, Clayton, Custer, DeLamar, Dewey, Rocky Bar, Atlantic City, Triumph

MONTANA

Western Ghost Towns	Ghost Town Album
Bannack	Giltedge
Bearmouth	Kendall
Beartown	Maiden
Clancey	
Elkhorn	
Garnet	
Granite	
Keystone	
Laurin	
Mammoth	
Marysville	
Melrose	
Philipsburg	
Rimini	
Southern Cross	
Virginia City	
Wickes	

Landusky, Castle, Hecla, Yogo Gulch, Ruby, New Year, Barker, Confederate Gulch.

NEVADA

Western Ghost Towns	Ghost Town Album
Austin	Washoe
Belmont	National
Candelaria	
Dayton	
Eureka	
Fairview	
Galena	
Goldpoint	
Goldfield	
Goodsprings	
Hamilton	
Manhattan	
Midas	
Nelson	
Pine Grove	
Rhyolite	
Rochester	
Tonapah	
Tuscarora	
Unionville	
Virginia City	

Jarbridge, Ione, Aurora, Berlin, Delamar, Ophir, Osceola, Palisade Queen.

NEW MEXICO

Western Ghost Towns	Ghost Town Album
None	Tyrone
	Magdalena
	Kelley
	White Oaks
	Kingston
	Lake Valley
	Hillsboro
	Pinos Altos

Elizabethtown, Mogollon, Alma, Shakespeare, Dawson, Madrid, Albemarle, Cimarron.

OREGON

Western Ghost Towns	Ghost Town Album
Antelope	Auburn
Austin	Malheur City
Bonanza	Lone Rock
Bourne	Richmond
Cornucopia	Sanger
Granite	
Grandview	
Greenhorn	
Hardman	
Hoskins	
Jacksonville	
Kerby	
Marysville	
Shaniko	
Sumpter	
Whitney	

Ashwood, Galena, Susanville, Promise, St. Louis, Willow, Shelburn, Ortley, Applegate.

SOUTH DAKOTA

Western Ghost Towns	Ghost Town Album
None	Hill City
	Custer
	Cascade Springs

Deadwood, Lead, Plumas, Trojan, Preston, Mystic, Galena, Rockerville, Rockville.

UTAH

Western Ghost Towns	Ghost Town Album
None	Bingham Canyon
	Alta
	Mammoth
	Park City
	Eureka
	Silver City

Fairfield, Hanna, Jericho, Mercury, Tablona, Silver Reef.

WASHINGTON

Western Ghost Towns	Ghost Town Album
Blewett Pass	Northport
Copper City	Bossburg
Index	Republic
Liberty	Orient
Skamokawa	Curlew
Sultan	
Trinity	
Wilkeson	

Conconully, Ruby, Nighthawk, Oroville, Monte Cristo, Galena, Garland Springs, Holden, Oysterville, Frankfort, Deep River, Macgowan.

WYOMING

Western Ghost Towns	Ghost Town Album
Atlantic City	Encampment
Diamondville	Battle
South Pass City	Rambler

Opal, Medicine Bow, Carbon, Glencoe, Dennison, Du Noir, Gold Hill, Miners Delight, Viola.

BRITISH COLUMBIA

Western Ghost Towns	Ghost Town Album
None	None

Allenby, Copper Mountain, Coalmont, Granite Creek, Tulameen, Barkerville, Cottonwood, Beaver Pass, Stanley, Ashcroft Manor, Cache Creek, Yale.